CRUISE
CONTROL

CRUISE CONTROL

understanding
sex addiction
in gay men

Robert Weiss, L.C.S.W., C.A.S.

ALYSONbooks

Cruise Control

Copyright © 2005 by Robert Weiss

First Edition: July 2005

Published by Alyson Books
245 West 17th Street, Suite 1200, New York, NY 10011
www.alyson.com

ALYSON *books*

Library of Congress Cataloging-in-Publication Data
   Weiss, Robert, 1961–
      Cruise control : understanding sex addiction in gay men / Rober Weiss.—1st ed.
      Includes bibliographical references.
         1. Gay men—Sexual behavior. 2. Gay Men—Psychology. 3. Sex addiction.
   I. Title.
   HQ76.W395 2005
   306.76'62—dc22   2005043622

ISBN-10: 1-55583-821-9
ISBN-13: 978-1-55583-821-8

10 9 8 7 6 5 4

Cover photography by Dwight Eschliman/Photographer's Choice Collection/Getty Images.
Cover design by Matt Sams

Printed in the United States of America
Distributed by Consortium Book Sales and Distribution
Distribution in the United Kingdom by Turnaround Publisher Services Ltd.

To those men searching among shadows for light

CONTENTS

ACKNOWLEDGMENTS

This book would never have been written without the ongoing encouragement and support of Jennifer Schneider, Jon Westerman, and Patrick Carnes. Thank you. I owe unending appreciation to Michael Alvarez, John Sealy, Sharon O'Hara, and Beverly Mitchell, who nurtured me and helped me to define my clinical skills and professional path. Thanks to those who have personally or professionally propped me up: Karen Kass, Alex Katehakis at SRI, Nick Street at Alyson Books, and my agent, Edite Kroll. Thanks also to Robin Cato, SASH, Jane Nunez, David Burke, and my skilled reviewers: David Bissette, Jes Montgomery, Dan Dudak, Joe Kort, Joni Lavick, and Deborah Corley.

FOREWORD

The experience of oppression generates self-doubt, fear, and shame in the lives of those affected by it. These internal psychological dynamics are at the core of addictive disease and compulsive behavior in general. And they become even more deeply rooted when the focus of oppression is human sexuality.

It's important to realize that sexual oppression is really another form of sexual abuse. In that sense, homophobia is about more than just prejudice. The oppressing culture is actually damaging to a gay man's emerging sexual self—a natural human process that's difficult even under the best of circumstances. Considering the violent feelings that motivate those with a homophobic social agenda and the vulnerability of the self during the process of sexual maturation, it's not a surprise that compulsive behavior is a problem for many gay people.

Readers should note that compulsive sexual behavior takes different forms. When it is excessive and self-destructive, we use the language of "addiction" to describe the pattern of behavior. When it takes the form of deprivation—of a withdrawal from sex and sexual connection—the illness is in its "anorexic" phase. Some people "binge and purge," alternating between either extreme. These cycles of sexual bingeing and purging can last a day or a decade.

Recovery from this illness means some people have to emerge from their avoidance and others have to recognize their addiction to high-risk and excessive behavior. Thus, the real challenge for both groups of people is reclaiming their sexual health—a process that is at the heart of this book.

Some people see the process of behavior modification in sexual recovery as an attack on gay liberation. They imagine that any effort to limit or alter gay sexual expression is an extension of the beliefs of those who are intolerant of sexual differences. These critics misjudge the process of sexual recovery as much as those who condemn any form of sex outside the traditional limits of heterosexual marriage.

In reality, many mental health professionals have worked diligently with their patients to help them learn to express their sexuality fully as well as to acknowledge sexual behaviors that are ultimately self-defeating. Neither extreme—an unquestioning belief in the exclusive sanctity of heterosexual marriage or an unconditional commitment to all forms of gay sexual expression—promotes true sexual health. As science helps us to understand the nature of addiction, it becomes increasingly apparent that both heterosexist oppression and reactive notions of sexual freedom account for the persistence of sexually addictive behavior among gay people.

We have needed a book and a voice to bring clarity to this very complicated issue. I believe we have both in *Cruise Control*. Robert Weiss carefully traces the various ways the misinterpretation of addictive behavior has caused suffering among gay men. Furthermore, he clearly understands and explains the pattern of bingeing and purging that characterizes the problem of sexual addiction. He is an empathetic guide through the proven strategies that have helped countless gay men develop healthy approaches to sexual expression amid the challenges and possibilities of the gay community.

I have known Rob Weiss since he was a young clinician. His ability to get to the heart of the problems presented by his patients was already legendary early in his career. Today, Rob has his own clinic, the Sexual Recovery Institute in Los Angeles. Through the institute he has established a national reputation for helping patients begin their sex addiction recovery, and many inpatient facilities routinely use the treatment plans developed by the institute as part of their aftercare recommendations. The gift of this book is to make Rob's wisdom and the resources of the Sexual Recovery Institute available to recovering communities and gay communities everywhere. It should find a place in the personal libraries of all of us who want to illuminate the dark recesses of our sexual selves in order to flourish as human beings.

Patrick Carnes, Ph.D.

CHAPTER ONE
AM I A SEX ADDICT?

Ed cruises the locker room long after he has finished his workout. Sex is always the "reward" he gives himself after a hard day and a rigorous gym routine. First on the workout floor and later in the locker room, he is always searching for—and usually finds—willing sex partners.

Pacing himself through his workout, Ed surveys the selection of bodies arrayed on the gym floor around him. Crotches, biceps, thighs, pecs, and faces all get instant mental ratings. The object of Ed's hunt is any attractive man who returns his gaze with equal interest and intensity.

Ed's cruising produces a physical reaction in him: his heart races, he feels slightly dizzy, and his desire to spot, evaluate, and pursue his "quarry" is an instinctive impulse.

He knows and easily recognizes all the signs of interest—the gaze, the nonverbal come-on, the postures and poses that acknowledge his attention. Once Ed makes a connection, he and his trick follow each other into a bathroom stall, the showers, or the steam room. The men pretend to relax in the sauna while they casually masturbate or flash their semierect penises to each other—and anyone else they might want to attract. Ed can quickly shift into a "detached mode" when he wants to avoid attention, then back to arousal in seconds.

He also knows the cues that will alert him if gym security is coming through to do a check. Sometimes he finds himself in the locker room for hours past his workout, cruising some of the men who meet his gaze but mostly just waiting for the right one to come along. He might lounge for long stretches of time in the sauna or make a protracted circuit between the whirlpool, steam room, and shower. He watches the regular patrons enter the locker room, clean up, and leave.

And still he waits. As the hours wear on he often says to himself, *Just a few more minutes and I'll leave,* or *When I get hungry, I'll go.* His most common mantra is *Just as soon as the right hot guy comes along I'll be done here.* But he invariably finds some reason to stay and look just a little bit longer.

Many of Ed's long evenings at the gym begin with just a peek around the locker room "just to see who's there"... only to end at midnight when the building closes. Once he's in "cruising mode," no matter how tired he is, Ed can't stop. He can't abandon the search until he has an orgasm; only then can he go home, exhausted but no longer obsessed.

Sex is always part of Ed's day, whether he's masturbating during his morning shower, cruising the nearby mall or corporate-park restrooms during lunch, or engaging in his postworkout gym ritual. Getting home before 10 on a weeknight or having no weekend plans usually means going online to hook up with strangers he meets on bulletin boards, in chat rooms, or by dialing onto phone sex lines. He often spends whole weekends either searching for sex partners or having sex.

In his rigidly compartmentalized daily sexual activities, Ed reveals a part of himself that his friends and coworkers most likely wouldn't even recognize. In toilet stalls or alleyways—for three minutes or three hours—he cruises other men, objectifies them, and has nameless, wordless sex, all the time experiencing extreme emotional arousal and physical intensity. Moments later, back on the job or at the dinner table with friends, no trace of his sexual exploits is apparent in his mood or demeanor. It's as if there are two versions of the same guy—one known to his friends and coworkers, the other a stranger.

Also unknown to friends are the many consequences of Ed's sexual adventures. An arrest for lewd conduct in a park bathroom a few years ago sent Ed scrambling to scrape up money for a lawyer and bail; he was too ashamed to ask anyone he knew to help out. Although he will never forget the humiliation of being handcuffed to a park lamppost while the police went looking for more people to arrest, Ed is even more pained when he recalls "finding himself" returning just a few weeks later to look for sex in the very place where he had recently been arrested.

And of course there are the STDs: rounds of venereal warts, bouts of syphilis, and the endless HIV tests. Late nights at the gym, evenings of online sex, or weekends at the sex club kept Ed frequently running late for appointments or work, which took a toll on his career. Twice in the past year, Ed's supervisors confronted him for being out of the office too much and for being late on projects.

He began to feel depressed and irritable, though he was unable to figure out the source of his distress. To good friends Ed confided that he wanted a relationship, but he complained that he could never find the right guy. In reality, several interesting guys stopped dating him when they found him unreliable about making dates or being on time. One man he really liked caught him flirting with and cruising someone else at a party and dropped him right then and there. Ed was 34 at the time, and it had been almost seven years since he had been in a serious relationship. Even though at times he still enjoyed being the "bad boy," it was getting more difficult to blame anyone but himself for his loneliness and increasing anxiety.

Despite these warning signs, it never occurred to Ed that his sex life might be the source of his problems. For Ed, it was easier to believe that fundamentally there was just something wrong with him as an individual—to believe that he was somehow defective. Sometimes, he even blamed his unhappiness on being gay; at such times he would tell himself, *That's just the way gay life is.*

Still, as an out gay man fully committed to open sexual choices and experiences, Ed became annoyed whenever anyone suggested that he might consider modifying his sexual behavior. His early confrontations with the homophobic attitudes of his conservative family and childhood community made him bristle all the more at the idea of restricting his sexual freedom. Certainly, the urban gay male culture that surrounded him fully supported his sexual exploits as long as the sex was safe (and for some of his peers, even that wasn't too important). Since he didn't talk about his sexual behavior, even with good friends, he received no feedback that might challenge the wisdom of his late-night exploits or the dangerous possibilities inherent in his brushes with the law and his health concerns. He just kept it all to himself.

Though adamant in his liberal beliefs about gay sex, Ed had seriously considered changing some of his sexual conduct after he repeatedly felt bad after engaging in certain activities. Many times Ed had said to himself, *This is the last time I am going to spend most of the weekend online looking for sex,* or *Okay, from now on, I will never have unsafe sex,* or whatever his troubling sexual activity was at a given moment. Sometimes these promises would take root for a time and he would stop. A new boyfriend, a new job, or an expensive purchase would excite him and temporarily divert his attention from his sexual patterns.

For a while Ed would feel hopeful and believe that he had put his bad feelings and problem behaviors behind him. Then one night or afternoon, often when he wasn't even expecting it to happen, he would "find himself" on the phone setting up an appointment for a "sensual massage" or going off to the sex club after a late evening out with friends. And there he was, at it all over again. After enough of these false starts and disappointments, he began to lose respect for himself and to feel deep frustration at his lack of self-will.

After years of compulsive sexuality, aching loneliness, escalating depression, and the stresses of living a double life, Ed was getting tired, yet he couldn't quite figure out what was wrong or exactly what to do. Though he had a good job, some supportive friends, and had even gone to therapy on and off, Ed just wasn't able to find a way to enjoy his life or be happy.

SEX ADDICTION IS NOT REALLY ABOUT SEX

Ed's story highlights many of the issues and experiences that are common to all sex addicts. A life constructed to maximize sexual opportunity, sharply compartmentalized modes of relating (to friends, family, and coworkers in one mode and to sexual partners in another), and serious consequences (legal and health-related) associated with sexual activities are all signs of a real problem.

One experience familiar to most sex addicts is the "trance" or "intensity" state, which propels the cycle of their sexual exploits. Much like the addictive gambler who sits at the card tables for hours, lost in the spell of playing the game, sex addicts can spend long periods of time in a trancelike state of physical and emotional stimulation. As in Ed's case, hours can vanish while the sex addict sits in a bathroom stall, cruises in a car or sex club, loses himself in Internet chat rooms, or wanders back and forth in a public park after dark. No one else may even be there and none of the right guys may ever show up, but the sex addict persists, unable to let go of the fantasy that any moment the next hot sex partner might come along. His excitement may never take the form of actual erection or orgasm, but he is clearly in a state of physical and emotional euphoria. Heterosexual sex addicts who hang out in strip clubs, hire prostitutes, or engage in cybersex describe the very same experience.

Someone caught up in a behavior-based arousal addiction such as gambling or sex is not thinking rationally. The very process of becoming emotionally aroused leaves him disconnected from his capacity for clear decision-making and healthy modes of relating. In those moments, he is unaware of the consequences of his actions or their similarity to past disappointments; rather, he is singularly focused on becoming more absorbed in whatever exciting (and momentarily distracting) sexual activity is in front of him.

When we hear about a famous pop star getting arrested for cruising a cop in a restroom or a movie star exposed for picking up street prostitutes, most of us shake our heads and ask, "What was he thinking? With his money and looks he could have had anybody he wanted. Why would he put himself in such jeopardy?" A ravenous yearning for intense sexual distractions compels sex addicts to repeat behaviors that put them in problematic situations. In Ed's case, this yearning manifested itself in his spending more time in the search for sex than in the act of sex itself—looking, cruising, and searching for hours on end. If we could examine Ed during all the hours he spent prowling locker rooms, waiting for partners in a public restroom, or in online chats, we would find both his body and mind in an altered chemical state. Quite literally, he would not be himself.

THE NEUROCHEMISTRY OF SEX ADDICTION

When people are under the influence of alcohol or drugs, their perceptions change and their moods shift; consequently, their attitudes and choices are altered by the use of the substance. Some people engage in sexual activities when they're high that they would never consider when they were sober; others abuse their spouses; still others drive their car recklessly or strive to become the life of the party. Some people use alcohol or drugs as an excuse for behaviors they would have liked to engage in anyway; for others, the chemical alteration brought about by substance abuse becomes an end in itself. This is often the precursor to addiction.

It's easier to understand addictions to substances like cocaine or crystal meth than addictions to behaviors like sex or gambling. Substance addictions involve putting something foreign into your body—like a drink or a pill—whereas it can be harder to understand an addiction to something that you do. The reality is that *any highly arousing or intense behavior can become addictive for some people*, depending upon how it affects their brain chemistry.

People become addicted to a certain behavior because it induces chemical changes in the brain. These changes are just as powerful and intensely arousing to them as the high other addicts get from alcohol or drugs. Behavioral addicts then become addicted to the way that their fantasies and activities influence their own neurochemistry.

These powerful cocktails of distraction are made up of naturally occurring chemicals in the brain like adrenaline, serotonin, epinephrine, dopamine, and endorphins that produce different moods. Individuals become addicted to behaviors that enable them to alter their brain chemistry to change their moods.

In truth, people who are addicted to sex, gambling, and compulsive spending are just as addicted to drugs as their substance-abusing counterparts. By engaging in certain behaviors, they have found a way to manipulate the chemical production system in their own bodies to get high without having to rely on an external catalyst like alcohol, nicotine, or heroin—though some sex addicts may use those substances as well. The physiological and emotional responses to their addicting behaviors are identical to the drug addict's relationship to his substance of choice.

SIGNS OF PSYCHOBIOLOGICAL AROUSAL (CREATED THROUGH FANTASY AND CRUISING)

- Rapid heartbeat
- Dilated pupils
- Fast, shallow breathing
- Sweaty palms
- Psychological intensity or vigilance
- Narrowing of emotions and/or intense focus on one emotion or experience
- Intellectual detachment from important people, values, and events

SEX ADDICTION IS NOT ABOUT ORGASM

For sex addicts, the focus of all the ritual cruising, contacting, and engaging is not necessarily orgasm—though the fantasy of orgasm partially drives their obsession. While spending hours walking the floors of a sex club or surfing the Internet, many sex addicts are unknowingly working to maintain an optimal level of emotional and neurochemical stimulation. They often spend long periods just searching, without ever having an orgasm or even an erection. In fact, having an orgasm is not always a welcome or desired part of the process; once orgasm occurs, the game is over and a clearer (often unwelcome) perspective on the situation dawns. At this point, the sex addict is reminded of the late hour, the possibility of disease, the money he has spent, another night of too little sleep, or promises broken once again.

Regardless of his particular sexual interests, the sex addict's real goal is to maintain his state of emotional euphoria through fantasy and cruising. Many sex addicts describe this hyper-arousal state as being in "the trance" or "the bubble." They truly feel their impulsive and compulsive actions are out of their own control. Stan describes his experience this way:

> Sometimes I swear I'm not even thinking of going cruising after work. It's like my car "drives itself" to the park. Before I leave the office, I might begin to get into some fantasy about what I might find there or about the last guy I met cruising, and before I know it, just when I think I was just going to drive home, there I am, parking by the bushes where I always go looking for sex. And it doesn't seem to matter if I have plans or other things to do that after-noon; I just seem to "end up" there anyway.

Joe, another sex addict, describes the powerlessness he feels when he's caught up in the intense emotional high of his acting out:

> Sometimes at home online just checking e-mail or paying bills, I will say to myself, *I'll just go into a queer chat room or look at some porn for, like, 10 minutes—that's it. Then no more computer, then I'm getting offline.* But before I know it like two or three hours have gone by and I am still sit-ting there zoned out, staring at the screen. It's like I have been in a daze. Never getting anything done that I really should be doing. And this doesn't just happen to me once in a while; if it did, I wouldn't be so concerned. I will spend three to four hours

a night several nights a week, sometimes whole weekends cruising and masturbating online to images and fantasy. I can sit for so long in one place that my whole body gets cramped and I still haven't eaten or done any of my chores—I just sit there staring at that stupid computer. I feel like the Internet is taking my life away from me.

As is the case with men who obsessively cruise gyms and bathhouses, men who cruise the Internet induce this temporary, trancelike hyperarousal state and sustain it through visual and emotional fantasy. And just like their more "extroverted" counterparts, many Internet sex addicts experience either a letdown once they reach orgasm and their body returns to its normal state or they need to start their searching all over again.

THE QUICK HIT

Though long periods of cruising and sexual intensity are typical of sex addictioin, it is not always possible to spend hours cruising or indulging in fantasy. Some sex addicts, having limited time or resources, will engage in quick, intense hits of sexual acting-out, then return to whatever they had been doing previously. A trip to the adult bookstore or mall bathroom during a daily lunch break offers relief from emotional tension through anonymous sex; in this way, many sex addicts make sexual acting-out a part of their daily routine. Other addicts may routinely stop at the public park on their way home for a fast sexual jaunt. By carefully ritualizing their behavior, they're able to work around the obliviousness to the passage of time normally associated with the trance state (and still be home in time for dinner with a partner).

All active addicts are opportunists with predatory instincts. When practicing their addiction, they will take advantage of almost any opportunity to get a hit of their substance or experience. Ray relates one recent example:

> A few weeks ago I was in a restaurant with my lover and my sister having lunch when I noticed a cute busboy giving me one-too-many glances over the salad bar. As soon as I got a drift of where he was coming from, my mind left our conversation and I immediately started fantasizing about meeting up with him for sex. As we ate I kept looking over my lover's shoulder to catch the busboy's eye. Once I had his attention, I cruised him whenever he passed by and waited for the right moment to hook up with him. I don't know if anyone else at the table noticed how distracted I was, but I must have been pretty checked out; I don't really remember much of what my lover and my sister were talking about.
>
> Looking back, I see that I was so focused on how I was going to get in that busboy's pants that I didn't even stop to consider that I'd begun to see my family—the ones I love the most—as an obstacle to getting sex. As soon as I saw the busboy give me the look and gesture toward the back of the restaurant, I quickly left the table to join him in the men's room. Our whole sexual episode took no longer than 10 minutes from start to finish, but I went through an entire range of emotional and physical intensity. When I returned to the table I acted like nothing at all had gone on.

THE CYCLE OF ADDICTION

Specialists in addiction have determined that all addicts exhibit predictable patterns of thought and behavior that lead them to act out. Whether drinking, using drugs, or engaging in addictive behaviors involving gambling or sex, addicts move through identifiable stages. Understanding these stages allows us to help them begin to recover.

The diagram below provides a simple overview of the cycle of sex addiction.[1] All patterns or cycles of addictive acting-out begin with a desire to *control* strong feelings and culminate in some kind of *emotional release*.

Someone with an addiction problem develops his dependence (on sex, alcohol, heroin, etc.) in an effort to manage and contain difficult emotions that he does not have a more effective way to handle. For reasons that we will discuss in chapter three, all addicts have a difficult time managing their feelings. When he feels stressed by any difficult situation (work, loneliness, family issues, money) he will turn to using an external substance (alcohol, drugs) or engaging in an addictive behavior (sex, gambling, spending) to distract himself from what feels like an uncontrollable internal experience (strong emotions).

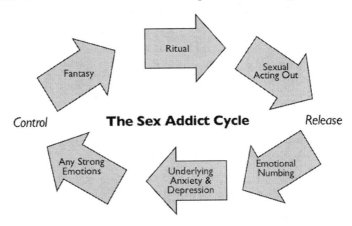

Simply put: Addicts use sex, food, gambling, alcohol, drugs, spending and other stimulating or numbing combinations in an attempt to feel better and have control over their feelings.

People with nonaddictive constitutions are often more keenly aware of their emotions and stressors and have better ways of managing them. By contrast, addicts are often not in touch with what they are feeling and therefore tend to be more *emotionally reactive*. When they're stressed or upset, addicts will impulsively turn to their addictions to distract themselves from difficult feelings with which they have no other means to deal. This pattern of utilizing substances or impulsive/compulsive behaviors or combinations of both to manage difficult feelings and events—rather than cultivating healthy habits of self-nurturing or asking for the support of caring others—is what addiction is all about.

Sex addicts use the intense familiar feelings provoked by sexual fantasy and sexual behavior to feel in control of deeper emotions, to feel powerful (when they feel vulnerable), and to feel desirable (when they're feeling needful). This pattern is the addict's default mode when he is stressed-out, angry, or simply when he wants to reward himself.

Let's look at the cycle of sex addiction in greater detail:

Any Strong Emotions: Feelings triggered by a bad day or a good day, seeing or talking to certain family or friends, financial or physical stress, or relationship problems can easily become greater than the addict can tolerate. He experiences more emotion than he can manage, but he may not consciously realize that he has reached the limit of his coping ability. Thus, he develops unconscious ways of coping with his difficulties.

Fantasy: In response to his stressful feelings and without other means to manage them, the addict begins to sexually fantasize.

He may think about the last sexual encounters he has had or imagine those that may lie ahead. He begins to plan a sexual experience and begins to actually feel the emotions he hopes to generate through the experience. As he fantasizes, his neurochemistry begins to produce the chemicals that a real sexual encounter would prompt; in other words, he becomes emotionally aroused by the idea of the sex. This arousal makes him increasingly less aware of the emotional stresses that triggered the fantasy, as he devotes his full attention to planning his sexual experience.

Ritual: Moved to action by his sexual fantasies, the addict begins to prepare for his sexual acting-out. He may change into more blatantly erotic clothing, call certain people he uses for sex, listen to specific music, head to the ATM for cash, or drive around his favorite cruisy neighborhoods. He may start searching online or pick up newspapers or magazines that feature ads for hookups or hustlers. Some addicts fuel their emotional excitement with drugs or alcohol (which also reduce the intensity of any distressing thoughts). Engaging in these presexual rituals intensifies his powerful emotional and neurochemical high and drives the addictive cycle forward.

Acting Out: Moments, hours, or even days into his fantasies and rituals, the sex addict arrives at the full-blown expression of his sexual behavior. This can include compulsive masturbation with porn, hiring prostitutes, paying for sexual massage, cheating, hooking up through phone or Internet chat rooms, anonymous or public sex, unsafe or multiple partner sex, exhibitionism, voyeurism, and any number of other behaviors, including going to adult bookstores, sex clubs, and bathhouses.

Release: Following his intense period of sexual acting-out, the sex addict experiences a sense of satisfaction through the release of much of the tension that had been building in his body and psyche. He may also feel emotionally numb, shameful, or anxious about the consequences of his actions. He may even have a desire to start the whole process over again immediately. He may say to himself, *This time it wasn't so bad*, or *I'll never do that again* in an effort to reduce the shame, anxiety, or fear he may feel around what he has been doing. After orgasm, some addicts experience an emotional reconnection with the problems they were trying to avoid when they entered the addictive cycle in the first place. Each sex addict has his own particular response to the cycle and his unique ways of gearing up for the next time.

Anxiety/Depression: All sex addicts harbor underlying negative feelings about themselves. When they're not in the "bubble" or "trance" that accompanies their sexually addictive cycle, they may look back with regret, fear, or anxiety about what they have been doing sexually and otherwise.

Some people suffer direct, unwanted consequences as a result of their sexual behavior, which makes them feel even worse. Since sex addicts act out in part to compensate for their limited emotional coping skills, as their sexual behavior and its consequences make them feel worse about themselves over time, the frequency and intensity of their behaviors may begin to escalate. They lose faith in themselves and turn more frequently to sex to try to feel better. The depression, shame, and anxiety generated by their sexual acting-out can often bring addicts back to the very need for emotional control that began the addiction cycle in the first place. Lacking a way out of the cycle, the sex addict repeats the very behaviors that produced his unhappiness and shame. This pattern can continue indefinitely or until some crisis causes the addict to seek help.

THE CYBERSEX-CYCLE

For addicts who hook up with sex partners through the Internet, impulsivity tends to drive sexual acting-out more than deliberate planning. Ken never consciously said to himself, *I am going to go out for sex today.* But a few moments of glancing at the local online bulletin boards or pop-up images on gay Web sites usually intrigued and aroused him enough to make him want to meet men for sex as soon as possible. Here are some typical online postings that would entice him.

- **Hot and Horny guy for afternoon sex—34 (Westside)**
- **Hot erotic massage with release—no charge—34 (Westside)**
- **I'M LOOKING – ASIANS AND LATINOS (Downtown)**
- **Blk bttm in need of some tops ASAP–29 (Suburbs)**
- **Young couple looking for 3rd, let's pnp, bb no prob. (Westside)**
- **26 y/o guy looking for f-buddy/laid-back friend**

Choosing from his cyber take-out menu, Ken would respond to two or three ads and then go to the gym or have a meal. By the time he got back to the computer, his sex partners were lined up and waiting for his response. While telling his friends that he really wanted to find a relationship, Ken never pursued online situations that involved anything more than sex.

On his way to hooking up he would tell himself that maybe "this time" the encounter would lead to more meaningful possibilities, but that never really happened. When the encounter was over Ken would often get down on himself: "I just gave myself away for nothing one more time." Or "the guy wasn't even that good looking but I did it anyway."

Regardless of these feelings, over time he "found himself" hooking up four to five times a week with guys he didn't know and whom he would never see again. He devoted less and less time to friends, work, and hobbies. Even when he said he was weary of feeling bad about himself and didn't want to meet men for casual sex anymore, the fantasy of who he might meet "this time" would eventually drive him back into his cycle. Again, as before, he found himself scanning the postings, getting excited about who was "out there," sending e-mails to prospective partners, hooking up for sex, and feeling depressed afterward. In coming chapters we will talk about specific actions addicts can take to break the cycle of impulsive cybersex activity.

BELIEF SYSTEMS AND IMPAIRED THINKING

All addicts—including sex addicts—develop distorted patterns of thinking and habits of denial that allow their dysfunctional sexual behavior to continue unchecked. Some forms of distorted thinking are simple rationalizations to keep looking for sex.

Rationalizations addicts use to justify sexual acting-out:
- I am just horny.
- Being around that cute guy all day made me want sex—now I want to go find someone that I can get off with.
- Sex is like getting a massage; it just helps me feel more relaxed.
- Sex is my reward after a difficult day.
- Lots of relationships get started through sex; maybe I'll find someone this way eventually.
- All my friends are getting laid; it's my turn to get some.

- When a guy doesn't cruise me, it just gives me reason to try harder to get him or someone else to have sex with me.
- I live alone—what else is there for me to do with my time?

Other attitudes used to sustain sexual acting-out are the by-products of broader belief systems. Sex addicts hold onto these to avoid feeling badly about their repeated patterns of sexual acting-out

Belief systems used to justify sexual acting-out:

- Being gay means having sex whenever, wherever, and with whomever I want.
- Why shouldn't I do this? Just look at how cold (unattractive, nagging, etc.) my partner is.
- Straight people are just naïve and reflexively conservative about sex. They would have sex all the time like us if they could.
- Who wouldn't have sex as often as possible if they were hot?
- I am more sexual because Hispanic/Jewish/ African-American men (pick any ethnicity) are inherently more sexual.

WHY ACT OUT?

A recent New York City study was conducted with over 180 gay and bisexual men who described themselves as being "sexually out of control." These men sought sex with other men mostly on the Internet but also in bathhouses, sex clubs, and public cruising areas. The men in the study reported having anywhere from two to over 400 sexual encounters during the 90-day period prior to their interview. During the course of the interview, the men offered many reasons for their "out-of-control" sexual behaviors. Their answers provide vivid insight into the belief systems, rationale, and frequent heartache of gay sex addicts. Researchers asked the men to respond to the self-reflexive question, "Why am I sexually out of control?" Their responses fell into three broad categories:

Internal Explanations

- **Low Self-esteem**: "I don't think much about myself and being with men sort of boosts my self-esteem."
- **Depression**: "I get very depressed ... and it gets to be too much and I act out."
- **Validation/Affection**: "I'm not getting the appreciation I need in my life ... so I use sex. It's like a substitute for love ... the easiest alternative to love is sex."
- **Stress/Escape**: "It's a great way of dealing with stress. Some people go out and have a drink ... it [sex] is a great relief for me."
- **Biological/Genetic**: "Too many hormones." "High sex drive." "Horny all the time." "The men in my family are all like this."

External Explanations

- **Relationship**: "I'm not in a relationship, and I like to have sex."
- **Childhood Sexual Abuse**: "I keep doing the same thing that was done to me."
- **Availability**: "I could find somebody every hour if I wanted to here in NYC."
- **Childhood Issues**: "My relationship with my father was nonexistent ... cruising is my way of searching for the love he didn't give me."

- **The End of a Relationship**
- **Catastrophes** (9/11, war)
- **Traumatic Life Events** (the death of a friend or loved one, loss of a job)
- **Seeing Attractive Men** (and not being able to deal with the impulse to have sex).
- **Drug and/or Alcohol Use**: Being under the influence triggers impulses to sexually act out.
- **Pornography**: Seeing porn triggers a desire to experience what was being seen.

GAY VS. STRAIGHT

Some common gay male cultural beliefs about sex make recognizing sex addiction in gay men more difficult than in straight men. Partly in response to the ongoing repression and abuse of gay men, Western gay urban culture encourages a wide range of sexual freedoms. While this is a positive response to living in a shame-based, homophobic culture, a counterculture of unfettered sexual expression can also serve to enable the denial of men who are locked into destructive addictive sexual patterns.

Gay male sex addicts are not compulsively sexual because of their sexual orientation but as a consequence of their individual psychological issues and neurological predisposition to addiction. This is exactly the same set of symptoms presented by straight male sex addicts. Unfortunately, for the gay sex addict, his increasingly destructive patterns of sexual behavior take place against a cultural background of dramatically greater sexual freedoms than those usually enjoyed by his heterosexual peers. The urban gay man is in some ways a prisoner of his own freedoms. He has fewer opportunities for self-examination and little support for behavior change when his associations to sexuality become obsessive.

SEX ADDICTION OR SEXUAL FREEDOM?

Not everyone who engages in anonymous sex, sees prostitutes, has multiple partners, is involved in the B/D-S/M or fetish scene, or participates in public sex is a sex addict. Not everyone who has affairs, unsafe sex, or keeps sexual secrets is a sex addict; indeed most people who fit these descriptions are likely not. The type of sexual activity you prefer, your choice of sexual partner(s), or where you go to have sex does not determine sex addiction. *Sex addicts are people whose lives worsen in direct relationship to their sexual behaviors,* though they may not even be aware of their diminishing quality of life and often struggle to conceal the extent or nature of their sexual activities.

Approximately 10% of gay men are sex addicts. This figure may seem low relative to some communities because gay sex addicts often surround themselves with men who are also acting out sexually. To most gay sex addicts, it looks like everyone out there is a guest at the never-ending party, having a lot of hot sex. Even addicts who isolate themselves or who rigidly compartmentalize their personal and sex lives still see a densely populated sex culture when they venture out to service their addiction.

Being a sex addict means that at some point you lose the ability to choose whether or not you are going to be sexual; in other words, you lose the ability to say no to your impulses and cravings. Repetitive and compulsive patterns of sexual acting-out begin to define who you are.

One way to understand sex addiction is to compare it to alcohol addiction or alcoholism. Many people drink alcohol—some frequently, some to excess—but their drinking in and of itself doesn't make them an alcoholic and their alcohol use does not present a problem in their lives because they can stop whenever they wish; they have choice. People who are alcoholics actually compose only a small percentage of the drinking population. Those who are alcoholics ignore or deny the consequences (arrest, job loss, health problems) of their drinking and often hide the extent of their drinking activities from friends and family. What makes them alcoholic is that despite the obvious problems their drinking causes them, the alcoholic isn't able or willing to stop drinking.

Similarly, the sex addict doesn't see or denies the problems that his sexual activity is continuously producing in his life, maintaining his denial with many of the rationalizations and belief systems described above. And he is also either unable or unwilling to change his sexual behavior despite its consequences. While people who aren't sex addicts can choose when and where to be sexual, sex addicts are often preoccupied with and compulsive about their sexuality.

CONSEQUENCES OF SEX ADDICTION

Chronic sex addiction brings with it a variety of unwelcome consequences for the sex addict and for those close to him. While these consequences vary from individual to individual, there are some common themes:

Isolation: Frequent and persistent sexual acting-out leaves little time for socializing and relationships. Sex addicts frequently isolate themselves, spending long periods of time in sexual situations apart from friendships, dating, community activities, and family. They leave social situations early or arrive late or avoid them altogether, being more keenly focused on getting into or out of sexual opportunities.

Broken relationships: Sex addicts often lie, break promises, cheat, give partners diseases, and expect spouses to put up with unacceptable behaviors, thereby causing hurt, pain, and chaos.

They frequently lose the people they most wish to keep in their lives or live in relationships stunted by lies, mistrust, and duplicity.

Lost creative or play time: Sex addicts don't usually have enough time or sufficient focus to engage their creativity. They often become detached from hobbies, art, sports, or other forms of creative self-expression in the pursuit of sex.

Increased guilt and shame: In the truest part of themselves, most sex addicts don't feel good about their hidden sexual lives. Many of them desperately want to stop or change the nature of their sexual behavior, but they find they are unable to do so. They repeatedly break promises they have made to themselves or others. This hidden shame can manifest in chronic feelings of low self-esteem, worthlessness, or failure.

Physical health concerns: Active sex addicts often place themselves at risk for sexually transmitted disease. Because they are only partially conscious of their actions in the "trance" or "bubble" state, they also risk physical damage to their bodies when they engage in rough or violent sex. Desperate for a sexual high, they also sometimes place themselves in situations where they could get mugged or beaten up or gay-bashed. Sex addicts are often exhausted from living a double life; even the most dedicated gymgoer can end up wasted from too little sleep and poor self-care.

Legal problems: Sex in public restrooms and parks leads to lewd conduct arrests for many gay sex addicts. Sex with prostitutes and sex with minors, exhibitionism, and voyeurism can also lead to serious legal consequences. Sex offenders are placed on a national registry, which can pose serious problems in employment and housing.

Mental health concerns: Sex addicts live with the fear that others will discover their hidden sexual lives. Having little time to devote to intimate friendships and relationships or creative activity leaves important emotional needs unmet. Both the fear of exposure and the actual consequences of getting caught can produce chronic periods of depression and anxiety, chronic low self-esteem, loneliness, and involvement with other addictions. The constant need for sexual attention can make the inevitable facts of aging and other life transitions all the more difficult for sex addicts to accept.

Multiple addictions: Drug and alcohol abuse can lead to sexually addictive behavior and vice versa. Sexual acting-out at sex clubs and circuit parties puts highly addictive substances in easy reach of people already predisposed to problem behaviors. (More on this in Chapter Four.)

Career or job problems: The time and energy addicts must devote to acting out sexually often affects their job performance. Sex addicts are often tired, late to work, or take long periods out of the workday to have or pursue sex (online, in nearby cruising spots, or with coworkers)—all to the detriment of their educational or job goals and focus.

Lack of primary relationships: Sex addiction is an intimacy disorder. While many sex addicts long for a lover or spouse, they may have never had one or been able to keep one very long because of their sexual compulsivity and their underlying low self-esteem and shame. Sex addicts' relationships often lack intimacy, good communication, and healthy sexuality.

HOMEWORK: TAKE A SEXUAL INVENTORY

One of the best ways to identify whether sex addiction is a problem for you is to take an honest look at your own sexual history and add up the pluses and the minuses of your sexual behaviors and activities over time. By simply making a list of your sexual activities from as early as you can remember to the present you can gain a surprising amount of insight into your relationship with your sexuality.

When you're writing your inventory, clearly note any sexual behaviors that produced negative consequences and consider whether you continued to engage in these behaviors anyway. Remember that there are important differences between the mistakes of early casual sexual experimentation or the occasional problem relationship and an ongoing pattern of sex addiction. Remember too that coming out can produce feelings of shame and confusion around sex that later become more manageable. The shame we sometimes feel during the early stages of our identity formation as gay men is very different than from the shame that sex addicts feel following their repetitive sexual activities.

There are easily recognizable signs to let you know if you have a problem with sex addiction. The following self-test may help you begin to explore whether or not you have this problem.

SELF-TEST (G-SAST) FOR SEX ADDICTION

The Gay Male Sexual Screening Addiction Test (G-SAST) is designed as a preliminary screening for sex addiction.[2] The G-SAST provides a profile of responses that frequently help to identify gay men who have problems with sex addiction. Answer each question by placing a check in the appropriate "yes/no" column. Answering "yes" to three of more questions may indicate issues of sex addiction, which would likely require further exploration with a competent therapist.

❏ Yes ❏ No 1. Were you sexually abused as a child or adolescent?

❏ Yes ❏ No 2. Did your parents have trouble with their sexual or romantic behaviors?

❏ Yes ❏ No 3. Do you often find yourself preoccupied and distracted with sexual thoughts?

❏ Yes ❏ No 4. Do you regret losing long periods of your time to the hunt or search for sex?

❏ Yes ❏ No 5. Does your use of phone sex lines and online porn or hook-ups exceed the time you spend with friends and family?

❏ Yes ❏ No 6. Do your significant other(s), friends, and/or family ever worry or complain about your sexual behavior (not related to sexual orientation)?

❏ Yes ❏ No 7. Do you have trouble stopping your sexual behavior when you know it is inappropriate and/or dangerous to your health?

❏ Yes ❏ No 8. Does pornography, phone sex, cybersex, etc. occupy more of your time than intimate contact with romantic partners?

❏ Yes ❏ No 9. Do you keep the extent or nature of your sexual activities (not related to sexual orientation) hidden from your friends and/or partners?

❏ Yes ❏ No 10. Are you eager for events with friends or family to be over so that you can go out to have sex?

❏ Yes ❏ No 11. Do you visit sexual bathhouses, sex clubs, and/or adult bookstores as a significant part of your sexual activity?

❏ Yes ❏ No 12. Do you believe that anonymous or casual sex has kept you from having more long-term intimate relationships or from reaching other personal goals?

❏ Yes ❏ No 13. Do you have trouble maintaining intimate relationships once the "sexual newness" of your partner has worn off?

❏ Yes ❏ No 14. Do your sexual encounters place you in danger of arrest for lewd conduct or public indecency?

❏ Yes ❏ No 15. If you are HIV-positive, do you continue to engage in risky or unsafe sexual behavior?

❏ Yes ❏ No 16. Has anyone ever been hurt emotionally by events related to your sexual behavior? In other words, have you ever lied to your partner or friends or not shown up for an event or appointment because of your sexual liaisons (not related to sexual orientation)?

❑ Yes ❑ No 17. Have you ever been approached, charged, and/or arrested by the police or other security personnel as a consequence of your sexual activity in a public place?

❑ Yes ❑ No 18. Have you ever been sexual with a minor?

❑ Yes ❑ No 19. When you have sex, do you feel depressed afterward?

❑ Yes ❑ No 20. Have you made repeated promises to yourself to change your sexual activity (not related to sexual orientation), only to break your promises later?

❑ Yes ❑ No 21. Have your sexual activities (not related to sexual orientation) interfered with some aspect of your professional or personal life? That is, have you been unable to perform at work or lost a relationship?

❑ Yes ❑ No 22. Have you engaged in unsafe or "risky" sexual practices even though you knew they could cause you harm?

❑ Yes ❑ No 23. Have you ever paid for sex?

❑ Yes ❑ No 24. Have you ever had sex with someone just because you were feeling aroused

and later felt ashamed or regretted it?
❏ Yes ❏ No 25. Have you regularly cruised public restrooms, rest areas, and/or parks looking
for sexual encounters with strangers?

Having honestly answered these questions is a good starting point for self-examination and reflection. At this point you may have more questions than answers. Chapter 2 will offer a more in-depth look at the signs and symptoms of sex addiction and help to sort out the many issues that arise out of looking at these difficult problems.

CHAPTER 2
SEX ADDICTION: TAKING A CLOSER LOOK

"If I spend a lot of time out having sex, does that make me a sex addict?"

"If someone else doesn't like my sexual behavior, does that make me a sex addict?"

"My friends say, 'You're such a sex addict,' but I think they're just jealous of how much action I get. How do I know if I really have a sex addiction problem?"

Perhaps the best way to start identifying sex addiction is to look at what sex addiction is not.

MYTHS ABOUT SEX ADDICTION

Myth #1: Someone with good morals wouldn't have this problem.

You are not a sex addict because your morals or ethics differ from the so-called majority. In other words, you are not a sex addict because you have multiple partners and you don't choose monogamy. You are not a sex addict because you are gay and not straight. However, you may be a sex addict if your sexual behavior often takes you outside *your own* system of values and beliefs, leaving you feeling bad about yourself and your relationships with other people. Consistently going outside your own moral comfort zone in pursuit of a sexual high is one of the warning signs of sex addiction (more on this later).

It's important to realize that sex addicts don't betray their partners and loved ones or violate their own personal belief systems because they are immoral people. They are driven to acts contrary to their character by the compulsive and impulsive nature of addiction.

Myth #2: People who have good religious values and truly believe in God don't act out sexually.

No one becomes a sex addict because he doesn't have a sufficiently strong religious belief system. You aren't a sex addict because you don't have sex according to biblical scripture or because you don't follow the proclamations of religious leaders who say that one kind of sexual behavior brings you closer to God than another.

Likewise, you don't heal from sex addiction by going through a religious conversion. Recovery from sex addiction doesn't come about solely through dedication to prayer, meditation, or rigorous religious study any more than recovery from drug addiction can be accomplished just by those means. Recovery from sex addiction involves taking a hard look at yourself and your relationship to sex, deciding what does and does not work in your life, and engaging active help from other people who are in a process of change and healing. Spirituality or religion may be a part of that process, but as an integrated component, not as the sole element.

Myth #3: All gay men are sex addicts.

Sex and love addiction is not just a problem among gay men. These diagnoses are as widespread and problematic among straight men and bisexuals as they are among gays. Heterosexual sex addicts act out in many of the same ways gay men do; they just act out in different settings and choose women rather than men to play with. Gay men go to sex clubs; straight men go to strip clubs. Gay men go to bath-houses; straight men hire prostitutes and meet them in motel rooms. Both gay and straight male sex addicts may end up at adult bookstores.

There is plenty of acting out among bisexuals and male-identified transsexuals as well. Straight male sex addicts act out through the same behavioral patterns and with the same degree of frequency, secrecy, and shame as their gay counter-parts. In 12-step meetings and group therapy for sex addic-tion, gay and straight men often recover side by side. In dis-cussions about their sexual experiences and their feelings about their addiction and recovery, the similarities between gay and straight sex addicts are much more apparent than their differences.

Myth #4: Sex addicts are sex offenders.

Sex offender is a legal term to describe someone who sex-ually forces himself on someone else without that individual's knowledge or consent. Rape, child molestation, and sexual battery are violent sex offenses and therefore are treated as felonies. Exhibitionism, voyeurism, and frotteurism (touch-ing the body parts of another individual without permission) are also considered actionable offenses, though in court they carry a lesser misdemeanor charge.

While some sex addicts—both gay and straight—may cross the line into offending behaviors, the vast majority of sex addicts never commit sexual offenses. The sexual behav-ior of a sex addict is not remarkably different from the behavior of most people who are not sex addicts. However, sex addicts tend to have much more frequent sexual encoun-ters, and their sexual activity often involves far more risk-taking.

A word to those who sexually offend: While most sex addicts never cross the line into committing sex offenses, some—particularly those attracted to the highs associated with risk-taking—occasionally do. If you have crossed the line into problems like voyeurism, exhibitionism, or predatory sexual behaviors with vulnerable minors or adults, you deserve help. If you are motivated to get well and wish to alter your sexual patterns, you have taken the first step in your battle. Many of the techniques and supportive suggestions offered in this book are very useful to both sex addicts who have commited offenses and nonaddicted offenders. Please get as much help as you can from them and reach out to supportive professionals and 12-step recovery groups.

Myth #5: If you stop acting out sexually with men, you will become more heterosexually oriented.

This folly of this myth may seem quite obvious to gay men who are comfortable with being gay. But some closeted bisexual men and closeted homosexual men seek treatment for what they describe as "sex addiction" or attend 12-step programs for sex addicts because they hate the fact that they are attracted to and aroused by members of the same sex. The impulse behind their search for "treatment" is their internalized homophobia.

Often the only way men who haven't come to terms with their sexual orientation can tolerate their sexual feelings is to pathologize them. These men come to sex addiction treatment to eliminate their sexual acting-out—which, in their view, encompasses any sexual activity with other men. To put the matter another way: They want to "recover" from their desire for sex with men, which they label as "sex addiction." For these troubled men, the label "sex addict" is a safer way to manage the trauma of their unexamined sexuality than actually facing their own bisexuality or homosexuality.

Some of these men languish in tortured marriages or a series of unfulfilling heterosexual relationships while acting out anonymously or having ongoing discreet affairs with men on the down-low. All the while they hate themselves for not being able to "get sober," which for them means no longer desiring men or having fantasies about them, let alone engaging in sex with them.

Internalized homophobia has nothing to do with sex addiction, good therapy, or 12-step recovery. *Healing from sex addiction in no way entails trying to change one's sexual orientation;* more to the point, sexual orientation cannot be altered through sex addiction meetings or therapy.

A word to bisexual and homosexual men in heterosexual marriages: When you married, you likely took a vow to be faithful to your wife. If you are having sex with men and keeping this a secret from your wife, you're engaging in a form of sexual acting-out that can only end in tragedy, illness, and/or heartbreak. There are all sorts of ramifications for your wife and children (if you have any), if you were to be publicly exposed or if you inadvertently give your wife a sexually transmitted disease. The problem is not your attraction to men; your problem is your clandestine sexual acting-out, which compels you to lie to your wife and put her and other people you love at risk.

For men in your circumstances, there are many ways to respond to the difficult emotions you feel that are far healthier than leading a double life and risking public or private humiliation. Other men have discovered and implemented these healthy solutions to their problems and are living far happier lives. On the other hand, not acknowledging your sexual attraction to men or trying to "become heterosexual" are unhealthy coping strategies and setups for future tragedy.

Many men in your situation have gone through professionally recognized treatment and found ways to negotiate sexual practices that allow them to live without shame, secrecy, and heartache regardless of whether they choose to remain married. Investigating sexual recovery programs and getting in touch with licensed professionals who provide sex therapy are good ways to start this process.

Myth #6: Sex Addiction is a sign of some other mental illness.

Quite often in the recent past, men who had problems controlling their sexual behaviors were misdiagnosed by well-meaning mental health professionals, who sometimes prescribed medications to treat medical conditions the patients didn't have. Misdiagnosis isn't unreasonable; there are several major mental disorders that do present hypersexuality (having a lot of sex) as a symptom. For example, people who have bipolar disorder—formerly called manic depression—can be extremely seductive and intensely sexual when they're in the manic stage of their disease.

Frequent, impulsive sexual activity can also be a symptom of Adult Attention Deficit Hyperactivity Disorder (ADHD). Despite their problematic sexual acting-out, people who suffer from ADHD are usually not sex addicts. When their emotional state is stabilized with proper therapy and medication, their hypersexual behaviors usually disappear.

For some speed and stimulant abusers (meth users, for example), drug abuse goes hand in hand with intense periods of sexual activity, which sometimes lasts for days at a time (see chapter 4 for more about multiple addictions). But once he stops or slows his drug use, many crystal meth addicts have little interest in continuing the intense sexual hunt that was such an important part of their drug ritual.

Myth number 7: Being involved in B/D-S/M, the leather scene, cross-dressing, or a fetish lifestyle makes you a sex addict.

Our human forms of sexual and romantic relationship and expression are as diverse as the individuals involved in them. Informed sex therapists and professionals know it is more important to reduce shame and to encourage men with these interests to safely enjoy what brings them pleasure, rather than to apply negative labels.

Although these scenes do attract their share of sex and drug addicts, the simple fact that you enjoy living an "alternative sexual lifestyle" does not make you a sex addict.

Now that we've debunked the primary myths about sex addiction, how do we go about differentiating a sex addict from someone who is not? What makes a sex addict's behavior different from someone who just likes to have a lot of sex?

In his book *Don't Call It Love*, Patrick Carnes lists 10 key signs that indicate the presence of sex addiction. By using these signs as a jumping-off point, we can begin to develop a strategy of recovery.

IDENTIFYING SEX ADDICTION

1. A Pattern of Out-of-Control Sexual Behavior

A sex addict's patterns of sexual behavior are characterized by a lack of control. While a nonaddicted individual can quickly see how his behavior causes problems or has the potential to do so, the sex addict continues despite the risks. He has likely experienced trouble in his life as a consequence of his sexual activities, and he is just as likely to have downplayed his troubles, even if they have brought him or others physical or emotional harm.

He appears unable or unwilling to place boundaries around sex, even when those limits would keep him and/or others safe from the possibility of physical or legal jeopardy. The amount of sex he has, the physical intensity of the sex act, and the time he spends having sex or in the search for sex often exceed what he intended, though he will often vigorously defend his activities. Unlike healthy people who self-correct if realize they have chosen a sexually inappropriate or sexually excessive behavior, the sex addict will often return to that same behavior or worse.

2. Severe Consequences Due to Sexual Behavior

As we saw in chapter 1, the consequences of sex addiction run the gamut from emotional to relational, financial, physical, and legal. At this point we should look more closely at the emotional consequences.

A sex addict can experience *humiliation* when he wakes up on yet another weekend to find himself on the smelly mattress of an unknown tweaker; *despair* when once again he realizes that he has spent so much money on phone sex that he can't pay the rent; acute *fear* when he is on the way to the hospital, after having gone too far in a submission-domination scene played out while he was high on crystal. He disregards the risk of yet another sexually transmitted disease as he moves on to the next sexual escapade. Important relationships are lost as a result of his lying, sexual secrecy, betrayal, and broken promises. *Depression, isolation,* and *low self-esteem* develop from the countless hours he spends in front of a computer screen masturbating or hanging out in the adult bookstores.

Anyone can experience negative consequences that relate to sex; bad things sometimes just happen. But sex addicts are risktakers. The law of probability dictates that the more frequently you take risks, the more likely it is that you will reap severe consequences as a result of your sexual behavior.

A Realistic Word About Public Sex: Chances are that having sex in public places will eventually get you arrested. Restrooms in parks, university campuses, and malls are built and maintained to provide an essential service for children and adults, both gay and straight. A father visiting a public park with a young child may have only one option available to him when that child needs to use the bathroom, and he probably doesn't want to run into two guys getting it on.

While it's an indelible part of the mystique, history, and erotic literature of gay and bisexual life, the public sex environment is absolutely no place for anyone who has something to lose if he were to end up with a police record. Many gifted teachers, lawyers, physicians, and other licensed professionals have lost their right to practice hard-won skills or ended up spending thousands of dollars in court fighting humiliating convictions for this particular sexual thrill. While many gay men defend their right to be sexual wherever, whenever, and however they wish and condemn the entrapment tactics often employed by law enforcement, the fact remains that public sex is illegal and arrests are commonplace and degrading.

While a nonaddicted individual may enjoy the very occasional lunchtime dalliance in the corporate men's room, most sex addicts are strongly attracted to the extra intensity of public sex environments. They will repeatedly return to that behavior until they are arrested or assaulted or until they can no longer deny the problem underlying their increasingly obsessive activity.

3. The Inability to Stop Sexual Behavior Despite Adverse Consequences

Taken alone, a negative consequence (a frightening encounter in a public restroom, for example) from some sexual behavior is easy enough to dismiss as a random occurrence. But when that consequence is one of a number of such problems related to your sexual behavior and when those problems fail to bring on change, it's a likely indicator that you're suffering from addiction. Consider Denny's story:

Denny knew he had a lot to lose, but in his mind, his behaviors didn't seem that different from how they had always been. Successful and bright, he had always managed to pull things together and had that gift of being the right guy in the right place.

Having grown up with an angry alcoholic father, he learned at an early age how to look good on the outside and hide the chaos underneath.

From adolescence he had used a secret world of compulsive masturbation and sex with older men to soothe himself and bolster his self-esteem. Eventually, his obsessive scholastic achievement got him into college and away from home.

At 37, he had a beautiful life and was headed toward the top of his career. He was in line for a partnership in a law firm. Nearly eight years into a committed relationship, he and his partner, Ben, were discussing having a child. From the outside it looked like Denny had it all. Overachieving and driven—even obsessive—in the workplace, Denny could be arrogant and dismissive of others, but his supervisors usually forgave his behavior because of his excellent performance. The number of cases he could carry, the extra business he brought to the firm, and his natural talent as a lawyer made it easy for others to dismiss his faults.

Whenever he was working on a case pending trial, Denny put in 14- to 16-hour days, sometimes for weeks at a time, and expected the same level of commitment from those around him. He made little time for intimacy, friendships, or socializing, leaving that job to Ben.

He also continued to live the double sexual life he had begun as a teenager. Disregarding the risks, Denny frequently stopped in train station restrooms for sex when he returned home late at night. In these underground stations, exhausted from his arduous day, he cruised the toilets or jerked-off at the urinal until he found someone he wanted to get off with. More than once he arrived just in time to witness the police handcuffing men in obvious stings set up to arrest those involved in the public sex. He would thank God that he had not arrived just a few minutes earlier and swear to himself that he would never cruise the restrooms again.

Though he would often not return to his habit for many days or weeks, he eventually would find himself cruising the same toilets again.

On more than one occasion, an irritated spot in his groin or on his thigh sent Denny racing to the bathroom with a magnifying glass or to the doctor, fearful that he had contracted a venereal disease related to his frequent extracurricular sexual activity. Despite his entirely reasonable fear of arrest, disease, and the potential consequences to his career and home life, Denny was unable to stop his addictive pattern of sexual cruising and acting out.

After the inevitable lewd conduct arrest, he became even more secretive about his behavior. He managed to get his sentence reduced to a fine with no jail time and told no one about the event. Instead he chose to move his sexual activity from train station restrooms to adult bookstores. When he found himself in a sleazy bookstore during the birth of his first child, he finally realized he needed to get help—he could not stop his dangerous pattern of sexual behavior on his own.

Denny's experience highlights the fact that the prospect or even the actual experience of adverse consequences often does not stop a sex addict from acting out, though a traumatic event may temporarily change the rhythm or location of his sexual ritual. Often adverse consequences will send a sex addict into a "flight to health." This is a term used for people who have not dealt with their underlying emotional problems but who, in response to some kind of crisis or setback, decide to "take matters into their own hands." Usually, they make a lot of quick changes in their behavior that they hope will somehow "fix the problem."

Unfortunately, no matter how painful the consequences that may have caused the sex addict to swear off his behavior, his desire to act out is always stronger than his fear of emotional, financial, or physical harm. Eventually, without outside intervention, he will always return to his old patterns, often with even lower self-esteem for not having been able to stop himself.

4. Persistent Pursuit of Self-destructive or High-risk Sexual Behavior

Since sex addiction is about using the fantasies and rituals of sexual activity to self-induce a neurochemical high, the more intense and exciting the sexual behavior, the higher the high. Forms of sexual behavior that involve risk or danger rev up the neurochemistry of the brain and make an intense experience that much more exciting. Below are some of the ways that sex addicts introduce risk into acting out sexually and incorporate it into their addictive pattern.

- Illegal sex activity or sex offenses (hiring prostitutes; engaging in public sex, exhibitionism, voyeurism, or frotteurism; viewing or downloading child/teen porn; having sex with minors)
- Unprotected sex—including or even especially sex that increases the chances of receiving or transmitting HIV or other STDs

- Risking getting caught (sex with a friend's lover, a coworker, sex outside a committed relationship, sex in places where you can be arrested, sex where others may intrude and be offended)
- Unethical sexual acting-out (a doctor having sex with patients, a minister with parishioners, a lawyer with a current client)
- Life-threatening or dangerous sex (sex with threatening people, sexual behaviors that could cause physical harm or death)

A word about online child pornography: While the behavior isn't typical of most sex addicts, viewing and downloading sexualized images of children and underage teenagers or attempting to meet up with them is a compulsion for some people and will eventually get you arrested. While you may feel safe alone at home on your computer viewing these images, the reality is that the FBI aggressively monitors sex-related child images and those who view them.

If you are aroused by pedophilic images and are active in the search for those images online, you place children at risk by encouraging child pornographers (professional and amateur) to continue to create these scenarios, and you also place yourself at risk for arrest. It is not unusual for the police to show up with a warrant demanding your computer as evidence once they determine that you have a history of such viewing and downloads.

You will never know that you are being observed

until they knock on your door. No kidding. Many otherwise comfortable lives have been ruined through such arrests and subsequent legal procedures. If you find that you cannot stop viewing and downloading child-sex images on your own, take your computer out of your home and seek professional help as soon as possible.

5. Important Social, Recreational, or Occupational Activities Are Sacrificed or Reduced Because of Addictive Sexual Behavior

The sex addict who spends four to five hours a day online cruising for porn billboards looking for sex has little time left over for social activity. One of the first things to disappear from the life of an active sex addict is free time. Cruising online, along the street, or in steam rooms; having affairs behind your partner's back; or compulsively masturbating to porn—these things can take up a lot of time. Gradually, friendships, creative expression, and personal interests become marginalized as the sex addict becomes more invested in his addictive world. Alan put it this way:

> The people whom I eventually became closest to were the people in my addictive world. I mean, they could have probably set the clock at the adult bookstore by when I came in after my work shift. Over time they even left out a coffee mug for me. In between tricks or cruising, I would hang out with the staff while I was waiting to get ready to go at it again. They would encourage me when some guy would come into the movie booths that they knew was my type. These guys

became my "friends," just like a druggie hangs out with his dealer and other druggies. I became one of those guys who had a nodding acquaintance with men whose names I never really knew, but many of whom I had already had sex with at the bookstore, bathhouse, and shower at my gym.

Another gay sex addict had this to say:

No event was too important for me to miss, be late for, or leave early from if I had the chance to get laid. Often I would sit through dinners or events just waiting to be able to leave so that I could go out to the bar to meet someone. Eventually, some friends just stopped calling, and invitations just didn't come anymore. The people who stayed in my life pretty much knew me as unreliable, as my sex life took precedence over pretty much everything else. At work I was famous for my "late lunches" which usually meant that I had met some guy and was hooking up for sex somewhere, [that I was] too into it or too far from work to return on time, or sometimes too late to return to work at all.

For men whose lives have become increasingly wrapped up in sex addiction, there is less and less time for socializing or friendships. As a result, when they're not working, sleeping, or eating, most sex addicts spend their time either on the hunt for sex or recovering from the last sexual binge. This forces them into isolation and deprives them of the sustaining nurturance of intimacy and the ongoing support of loved ones.

6. Ongoing Desire or Attempts to Limit Sexual Behavior

People who are living in sexual health don't often desire to limit or change their sexuality. Most men, unless they are going through a period of physical change or emotional loss, speak of desiring more sex, not less.

The desire to limit sexual behavior sounds a bit like the desire to limit drinking. Most normal drinkers don't even think about limiting or changing their drinking patterns. It is a sure sign that an alcohol problem is looming when someone is actually thinking about limiting their drinking. Sometimes a sex addict will break through their denial either by crossing a sexual boundary he never thought he would or due to some negative consequence, like an arrest. At these times he may attempt to try to stop his problematic sexual activity behavior altogether (quit cold turkey) or limit his amount of sexual activity.

Some troubled sex addicts will simply try to change venues; they imagine this will solve their problems. For example, they will stop going to the places they can get arrested and only have sex in sex clubs or bathhouses, or they will stop looking online for sex and only go out to bars. Others will increase their masturbation and/or pornography use in an effort to control or reduce their contact with sexual partners. All these strategies are like changing deck chairs on the *Titanic*! The new situation may seem momentarily safer, but it eventually will end up the same.

7. Sexual Obsession and Fantasy Become Primary Emotional Coping Strategies

As we will discuss more fully in chapter 3, sex addiction is an unhealthy attempt to meet several profound emotional needs—most of which have nothing to do with sex. One of the primary functions of sex addiction is as a means to stabilize mood. For the sex addict, sexual fantasy and sexual activity, whether carried out alone or with a partner, provide excitement and distraction while allowing him to avoid life's emotional challenges.

Pain, anxiety, anger, fear, and frustration are blunted and discharged through hours of masturbation, cruising, flirtation, and sexual fantasy. In this way the addict avoids having to struggle with very human concerns like facing and resolving conflict, tolerating loneliness, the fear of building intimacy, and so on.

As a way to "check out," many sex addicts cruise or objectify every hot guy they see. While noticing or even being distracted by attractive people is a part of healthy sexuality, sex addicts tend to gawk rather than glance at handsome men. This is a form of obsessive distraction. Roger—whose partner has often asked him to stop ogling other men when they are together—describes his experience:

> One of the hardest things for me to understand and get under control was my constant staring at guys. At first I didn't even know that I was doing it. When Tony would say that my staring bothered him, I would insist that he was "making it up" or "just being jealous." Cruising someone over a friend's or a lover's shoulder just seemed natural to me, even if I was totally missing what they were saying. I just couldn't stop. In healing my sexuality I had to learn to turn away from this obsessive cruising because it upset people I cared about and fed my desire to sexually act out.

Sex addicts learn from their early life experiences that it is safer to turn outward to the hunt for sex to try to control their feelings than to reach out to others for support. Seduction and arousal become replacements for vulnerability and intimacy. Inner emotional conflicts are never fully resolved, and personal growth is not achieved. Sex addicts can always rely on the search, chase, and eventually the sex itself to temporarily ease their troubles. Having never learned how to tolerate the fears we all have about being vulnerable, sex addicts use sexual intensity to help them feel powerful and in control and thereby to escape feelings they don't consciously know how to manage.

8. The Amount of Sexual Activity or Intensity of the Experience Increases Because the Current Level Is Insufficient

Much like drug addicts who seek more drugs or more powerful drugs (or both) to maintain an emotional high, sex addicts may gradually find themselves engaging in sexual activity more often as well as getting involved in kinds of behavior they had never imagined themselves getting into before.

Again, this speaks to the brain chemistry involved in the addiction process. Over time it takes more sexual activity and more intensity to get the same high. What was once a few minutes on the computer once or twice a week before bed can become a nightly ritual involving hours of online chatting and masturbating. The occasional visit to the "sensual massage'" prostitute can become a regular weekly activity.

Unfortunately, for the sex addict, many of the same sexual activities that produce a profoundly intense high are the ones most likely to produce profound fear and shame when he objectively views them in the light of day. Sex addicts are doubly challenged not only because they engage in self-destructive and high-risk sexual behaviors, but also because they then suffer shame and self-hatred when they look back—post orgasm—and wonder what the heck they were doing and why. Since sex addicts lack healthy coping mechanisms to deal with challenging emotions such as shame and self-hatred, one familiar way to cope is simply to have more sex.

Now a professional counselor, Jason looks back on the ways sex addiction affected his value system and his life:

> In the early days of HIV prevention, I was very safe sex–focused. When I volunteered to help out at the local gay community center, I used to teach safer-sex behavior and dating classes. I couldn't even imagine a time when I would be out there having unsafe sex, and I would get angry with people who did.
>
> Yet over time, as I became more compulsively sexual, the relationship between my values, beliefs, and my sexual behaviors disintegrated. I became so desperately hungry for touch, for sex. I desperately wanted to be desired—to know that a guy wanted me—and at some point it didn't seem to matter what I did to get attention, especially if the guy was really handsome.
>
> In the sex clubs condoms came first of course—condoms, condoms, and more condoms. Then later it became exciting to me to start letting guys insert their fingers into me, letting fantasy do the rest. I enjoyed it, but I kept telling myself that I could just keep the desire for more in my mind as a fantasy, that I wouldn't go further, but the thoughts were there—of bare-backing, sex without condoms.
>
> Then I let someone enter me, but not to [the point of] orgasm, and even then only after he promised me that he was HIV-negative. I felt a lot

of shame after that time. But soon I did it again with someone else without even asking his HIV status, and I didn't feel so bad about it. A few weeks later I let someone come inside me. After that, I really didn't let myself think about it too much. The more I got into the unsafe sex, the less I let myself think about it. Once I started, though, it got very addictive very quickly.

Jason's story vividly describes the progression of sex addiction—how emotional needfulness can play out sexually, leading to the lowering of personal boundaries and a steady increase in sexual risk taking. He is describing his own denial and self-delusion when he recalls thinking that a powerful sexual fantasy wouldn't eventually be played out just because he vowed to himself that he wouldn't engage in it. His story shows how acting out powerful shame-based sexual behaviors becomes more addictive as the addict finds himself engaging in ever more extreme activity to block out the negative feelings that acting out produces.

9. Severe Mood Changes Around Sexual Activity

Another striking similarity between sex addiction and drug addiction is that when sex addicts begin to fantasize about the possibility of acting out sexually, they completely blank out on the problems that their sexual behaviors have caused them in the past. Once the fantasies start, it's like all the negative feelings and consequences of the past never happened.

Flush with excitement and anticipation, the addict eagerly plans and moves toward his sexual escapades in complete oblivion to the prospect of any problems down the road. Of course when the sex is over, the memory of past shame and confusion often can rush right back in.

Michael describes his sex/mood cycle this way:

Excitement Before the Sex...

It's a slow morning at my office. I am sitting at my desk and something triggers me—maybe a flirty phone conversation or getting the weekly arts paper or maybe thinking of a guy I saw walking out of the restroom on my coffee break.

Anyway, I will start fantasizing about sex. I start thinking about guys I saw yesterday at the pool or guys I saw in the gym shower. Then I try to come up with an image in my mind of a guy who turned me on—like some kind of online search engine in my head.

I begin to feel some excitement in my chest and tingling in my fingers. I start thumbing through the back pages of the arts paper, looking at the massage and escort ads. I go online to some sites and look at porn—all of this at work.

Now I am making a plan. I am going to call one of these guys, make a date, and go to his place when I get off. I start to dial numbers, being careful no one is around my desk to hear. I am totally into it. I get one guy on the phone: Greg. He will be home waiting for me and he is just my type. He describes exactly the kind of sex we are going to have. I can't wait till I can leave. I just have to get to the bank to get some money to pay him. This is exciting and makes the day so much better. I think of little else but getting out of the office, and the rest of the day flies by. I feel stimulated and motivated.

The Letdown After ...

What was I doing there? I can't believe I left work early, even though I promised my boss I would get some projects finished. My excuse was really lame.

Even though he was kind of cute, I think that guy had been up a few days; I could tell he was kind of tweaked. His house wasn't really clean and it didn't feel entirely safe there. Why didn't I just leave? I was excited, and he was attractive. I guess I wasn't really in a place where I could think a whole lot further than that.

But now I feel like shit—I can't keep doing this. For one thing, I don't have the money. For a whole bunch of weeks now I have been saving to get some important bills paid and now I am right back where I started. Besides, even if this had been an awesome experience—right guy, perfect location—I don't want to see prostitutes. I want to be wanted for me. Right now I just want to go home. I feel dirty, confused and disappointed in myself. I just want to shower and go to sleep.

Michael's story gives us an opportunity to see how the neurochemistry of sex addiction influences mood changes. Notice how in the beginning of his fantasy Michael's thoughts are all about excitement and positive thinking. He is feeling wanted, desired, and aroused. The intense anticipation of sex lifts his mood, but it also blocks out the facts that he doesn't really have the money to see this guy, that he has work responsibilities to fulfill, and that his real goal is to be wanted for himself, not to pay for sex.

This is in part what differentiates an addict from a nonaddict. A healthy man might experience the same fantasy arousal, but he would also be able to weigh the potential consequences and make a more balanced decision. Michael's decision is completely swayed by his feelings in the moment.

After the sex is over, Michael suddenly regains his awareness of the difficult facts of his situation and experiences shame and self-criticism for having acted against his best interests and personal beliefs. He feels out of control and over time comes to hate himself for it. The rush of the anticipation of sex has been replaced with self-reproach and self-hatred after the sex. This pattern is typical of sex addiction.

Acting outside your personal belief system in any important area of your life is going to make you feel bad. Whether you're treating a friend or lover unkindly, misrepresenting yourself to family or coworkers, or waking up from a sexual event wondering what you are doing and why you've done it, looking at yourself and not liking what you see inevitably produces feelings of low self-esteem, sadness, and ultimately depression.

Making repeated promises to yourself to change or stop unhealthy sexual behavior—only to return to it again and again—will only produce feelings of failure and hopelessness. These feelings will recur with increasing intensity each time you sexually act out.

10. Inordinate Amounts of Time Spent in Obtaining Sex, Being Sexual, or Recovering from Sexual Experiences

Because addictive disorders develop incrementally—worsening bit by bit over time—a sex addict often doesn't realize how much of his life has been taken over by his addiction.

Many of the testimonials from recovering addicts show how compulsively searching for and having sex begin to replace friends, intimacy, creative hobbies, and work achievements. Stopping this behavior dramatically reveals to the addict the portion of his life that he has devoted to cruising, cybersex, sexual intrigue, flirtation, sex parties, sex clubs, lost weekends, and the like.

And it's not just searching for sex and hooking up that take time. Being up most of the night looking for sex means you have to recapture sleep that has been deferred or finish work that might have been completed while you were acting out sexually. Sex addiction also takes a physical toll; maintaining good physical health—beyond a superficial concern for big muscles—becomes extremely challenging.

Later in the book we will talk about what to do with all of the time and energy addicts recover when they decide to change their behavior. For now, let's take a look at what drives sex addiction and what purpose it serves.

CHAPTER 3
HOW DID I GET TO BE A SEX ADDICT?

What draws people into a lifelong struggle with addictive substances and behaviors? Some researchers theorize that biological and genetic forces predispose people toward addictive problems (the nature argument). Others suggest that the forces that shape early childhood development and the experience of trauma lead people to use patterns of addictive behavior to help them of cope with life's stresses (the nurture argument).

Most likely, the development of addictive behaviors is influenced both by the early interplay between and combination of the influences of nature and nurture. Understanding the history behind your sexually addictive behaviors and the habit structure that supports them can help to reduce harmful feelings of shame and provide a road map toward healing. Realizing that acting out sexually serves as an emotional "survival" strategy to allow you to tolerate difficult emotions or experiences can help you feel less ashamed or "flawed" when you begin to examine the nature and history of your sexual activities.

This chapter will illustrate some of the psychological issues that underlie all patterns of addiction, with an emphasis on the specific concerns of gay sex addicts. Let's start off with some general questions regarding sex addiction.

GENETICS AND FAMILY HISTORY

"Addiction is a family disease," and many sex addicts report coming from families with histories of other addictions and emotional disorders. Eating disorders, alcoholism, workaholism, and drug, gambling, and spending addictions are common in the immediate and extended families of sex addicts. Recovering sex addicts who review their histories in therapy will often recall watching uncles, sisters, fathers, or other family members struggle with varying addictive behaviors and forms of emotional illnesses. Experts believe that addictions, for some people, develop as a means to "self-medicate" and/or manage underlying genetically carried emotional challenges.

Some people begin life less well-equipped to manage difficult stresses than others. This ability is, in part, a genetically influenced trait. The symptoms of undiagnosed disorders such as depression and anxiety can be masked and managed through patterns of addictive and compulsive behavior. Many sex addicts, having inherited some kind of genetic emotional imbalances, learn early to use fantasy and arousal to temporarily stabilize mood or to avoid anxiety. Later, as they discover sexual pleasure, fantasy takes on an even more powerful and distracting role, and addicts begin to lose themselves in it in a way that characterizes sexual acting-out.

SURVIVING CHILDHOOD

Marty, who's now in treatment for his porn and cybersex addiction, recalls that, as a child, he would often stare out his bedroom window for hours in an effort to tune out the sounds of his parents' endless fighting.

> I remember being six or seven and going to my window nightly with a pad and a pencil to tally up the types of cars going by. I taught myself to tell

the Ford Mustangs from the Camaros from the Civics just from the taillights. I could guess every type of car from my window, and each night I made it my job to check them out, testing myself to get it right.

Now, recalling it in therapy, I can still feel how that compulsive counting and watching distracted me from the shouting and the smashing things that was going on just down the hall from my room. Of course it makes perfect sense to me now that as an adult I have learned to distract myself by looking into the windows of cyber-porn or reading online sex bulletin boards, night after night, whenever I am feeling stressed out and need to get out of my feelings. It seems like I am still using many of the very same skills I learned to distract myself as a little boy—to soothe myself and escape.

All addicts reach for some external substance, experience, or both to help them cope instead of learning to rely on their own internal emotional resources. Families with addiction problems tend to pass on dysfunctional patterns of relating and managing stress and conflict. Children witness these problem behaviors in their caretakers—in the case of some kids, this abuse in its various forms is inflicted on them directly.

Recent research on childhood trauma and abuse suggests that the actual development of a child's brain is altered by severe or repetitive negative experiences and that later in life the victims of these experiences face ongoing struggles with anxiety, depression, or addictive behaviors. In the past few decades, researchers have developed prescription medications called SSRIs (selective serotonin reuptake inhibitors) that, along with other medications, have proved quite effective in relieving many symptoms of anxiety, compulsivity, and depression.

Some recovering sex addicts have found these drugs helpful in reducing some of their "drivenness"—the compulsive part of their sex addiction—as they worked on longer-term behavioral changes in the context of therapy, 12-step groups, and/or treatment programs.

While these medications are not a cure for a lifetime of addictive behaviors—they don't teach you anything about healthy coping strategies—they can help to alleviate some of the neurochemical imbalances that cause sex addicts to compulsively return to their problematic behaviors.

WHY USE SEX AS A DRUG?

Chapter one introduced the idea that sex addiction is not specifically about sex, but more about emotional arousal. Most sex addicts who've gained some insight into their behavior will tell you that the sex act itself is a relatively minor part of the entire experience. It's the planning, the chase, the cruising (people or images), and the fantasy that make the behavior so addictive. If sex addiction is not simply about having sex and reaching orgasm, what purpose do arousal, intensity, and excitement serve for the man who is repeatedly acting out sexual behavior that diminishes his quality of life and that can place him in physical or emotional jeopardy?

SEX FOR SELF-ESTEEM

Even the most self-destructive patterns of sexual acting-out serve a relatively useful psychological purpose in the stressful, shame-based, anxiety-driven life of a sex addict. Although the addict may view his behavior—obsessive cruising, flirting, anonymous sex, repeatedly hiring prostitutes, or compulsive use of phone/cybersex—as "just being horny" or as "a way to meet men" or as "just getting off," it really represents a desperate attempt to fill a well-defended emotional void hollowed out of loneliness, frustration, and low self-esteem.

The sex addict uses sex and romantic intensity to say, "Look at me! Pay attention to me! Notice me! Love me! Don't reject me! Need me! Desire me! Make me feel lovable! Help me to feel whole, even just for a few hours or moments." Every time he leaves his house, craning his neck to catch the attention of every attractive guy he sees walking or driving by, the sex addict silently screams out his need for attention, validation, and affirmation.

Steven describes his experience this way:

> I found a way to gain control over men from almost as early as I could remember, and I knew how to get them to notice me. From my first sexual encounters in New York City subway tearooms at 14, I quickly learned how to be seductive and get the attention I craved (and that I wasn't getting at home). Whether I was working some of the queer teachers at my high school for "special attention" or cruising fancy Manhattan department stores seeking some daddy to take care of me, I knew that once I could get a guy to look at me with lust, I had some power over him.
>
> Lord knows my home life was out of control and as crazy as could be. There was no way for me to get much of anything there. But when I hit the streets, cruised the glory holes in the public restrooms, or worked the bars, even though I was only

a kid, I felt in control especially when I could get grown men to totally want and desire me.

The situation was particularly good if I could get these older men to think that they were special. Then they would invite me to their houses and give me things—house keys, cash, gifts—that made me feel important.

Sex addicts use seduction and sex to resolve unmet emotional needs, which is what distinguishes the psychology of a sex addict from that of a healthier individual. The healthy, horny guy just doesn't have as much emotionally invested in his sensual and sexual interactions as the sex addict. The nonaddict may cruise, flirt, have anonymous sex, and all the rest, but he isn't driven to his behavior by a deeper longing for constant self-validation. And he doesn't need to repeat the sexual behavior over and over again to make himself feel okay (though he may choose to return to certain behaviors because he enjoys them recreationally).

It doesn't seem to matter whether the sex addict is in a relationship or single, whether he has many friends or is socially isolated. No matter how much traditional love and support might be available to him, without taking specific actions to address his inner deficits, he will continue his hunt for the next guy to notice and want him—and the next and the next.

USING SEX TO COPE

The sex addict pursues his ritualized sexual patterns in order to "get out of himself" and escape what he is feeling rather than simply "to have a good time." Alan, now in his third year of healing from a lifelong history of anonymous cruising and over a thousand sexual partners, put it this way:

I used to see my work travel schedule as an ideal way to have a fun sexual life. My job took me out on the road a couple of times a month, and I often wouldn't get much farther than the airport terminal men's room before I was cruising, flirting, and looking for instant intimacy, attention, and sex.

I can't think of a trip I took in five years of business travel where I didn't find at least one anonymous partner—often more. A free evening on the road always meant going to the local bar or sex club or getting a sexual massage in my hotel room. Getting into treatment and recovery helped me realize that underneath all my frenzied sexual activity were a lot of difficult feelings about leaving home and traveling all the time—emotions I never knew I even had.

All that compulsive cruising and sex was covering up deep feelings of loneliness and sadness. Before I got into recovery from sex addiction it never even occurred to me that it was just plain hard on me to be on the road so often, that I missed my friends, my family, my home. Looking back at my behavior now I can see that what I was thinking was a hot, good time was literally my attempt to never have to feel any unhappiness.

I'm not saying that I didn't have some good times and even some hot sex. But what was wrong with it for me was that over time it didn't feel like I really had a choice. It became so automatic. The flirting, cruising, and sex was as much a part of my work life as eating and sleeping. Ultimately, it became less about having a good time and more about just getting it done.

> Honestly looking back, I spent a lot of time man-hunting till all hours and being with people I didn't really want to be with, but settled for. There weren't too many occasions when I actually got some prize stud in bed for the evening.

The psychological issues underlying Alan's sexual acting-out presented themselves in treatment after he made a commitment to stop his addictive sexual behavior. Alan's therapy helped him understand that the experience of having been a latchkey kid and the child of a very unhappy divorced home at an early age was still affecting him as an adult. Left alone to take care of himself and having to tolerate loss and loneliness when he was too young to manage those feelings, Alan never developed the skills to handle his feelings of abandonment when they arose in his adult life.

Though charming, seductive, and socially skilled on the outside, Alan remained on the inside a lonely, frustrated little boy who used his social skills to get the attention and validation he craved through flirtation, cruising, and sex. As long as he continued to use sex as a salve for his emotional pain, he had no way to begin to grow.

Using sex as a way to cope or self-medicate has different childhood origins and serves different purposes for different people. David, a compulsive masturbator and cybersex abuser, established a pattern of masturbation in early childhood that continued into his adult life:

> I was 8 when my mom left and didn't come back. She had been drinking on and off pretty heavily since I was really little. I remember her yelling, throwing things, and then crying until she fell asleep.

I would comfort her at times, bringing her my blanket as she lay passed out in the living room. When she wouldn't wake up for long periods I learned to feed myself and wash up on my own.

When she was mad at me, Mom would make me stand in the corner naked—I still remember the feelings of humiliation and unfairness. After those times I would go into my bedroom, lie on my stomach, and rock back and forth to comfort myself. I learned that by rubbing my penis on the sheets I would get a pleasurable feeling and start to feel better.

I learned early on that masturbation was a way to soothe myself and I started doing it all the time. By adolescence, spending hours in my room masturbating to porn was a daily ritual. It seemed like most of my friends were doing it, so I was cool with it.

But by the time I reached out for help, at 34, I was masturbating nightly to get to sleep and also most mornings in the shower. Some days I masturbated to the point of injury, but even that wouldn't stop me. I had a porn collection locked in my desk drawer at work so that I could masturbate in the restroom on my lunch break. I spent most weekends and evenings online with porn, in chat rooms, or hiring a prostitute/masseuse to come to my apartment for sex.

My sex life with guys I actually liked was practically nonexistent. I never really developed the skills or the faith in myself that would allow me to carry out a meaningful, longer-term relationship. Eventually I had practically no social life, few loving relationships, and even less hope.

David learned early in life that he couldn't turn to the loving support of family relationships for soothing and comfort. Overwhelmed, fearful, and too young to know how else to soothe himself, he discovered in early childhood that masturbation and fantasy were effective ways to cope with and medicate his emotional pain.

The key thing to David's story is not only that he learned early to use masturbation for the physical pleasure it gave him, but also for the self-sustaining comfort and distraction it offered. This early pattern of distraction and arousal became such an integral part of his life that as the years went by he wasn't able to see the toll it exacted on his time, emotional health, and prospects for intimate relationships.

As his sexual behavior evolved into an all-consuming sex addiction, David's emotional growth was stunted, much as excessive drinking stunts the personal growth of an alcoholic. Only by ending his compulsive masturbation; seeing and grieving his traumatic childhood in therapy; and building new coping mechanisms was David able to finally move on.

Note that David's very real problem with sex addiction only occasionally involved sex with other people. He didn't have many partners, nor did he ever put himself in any serious physical or legal jeopardy. David's addiction-related losses and unfortunate consequences were directly related to the countless hours he had devoted to his sexual behavior, the isolation that it produced, and the hopelessness he felt when he came to believe that he was not deserving or capable of love.

ABUSE PLAYS A PART

Whenever someone begins to explore how he ended up as a sex addict, he often wonders whether the roots of his addiction lie in childhood abuse. "Did I become a sex addict because I suffered physical or sexual abuse?" or "Did I become a sex addict because I watched my mom drink and fight with my Dad all the time?"

What role does childhood neglect and abuse play in the psychological makeup of someone with a sexually addictive disorder? Many gay men who decide to do something about their sexual acting-out later realize that painful childhood issues are contributing factors to their addiction.

But as long as addicts remain locked into their numbing and shaming patterns of active sex addiction—with the requisite drama of disease, intrigue, multiple boyfriends, drug use, arrests, and betrayal—it is not possible for them to examine the past and discover how these patterns emerged from their early challenges. *Sex addicts need to stop acting out before they can truly come to terms with their past.* Many recovering sex addicts who have spent years in psychotherapy prior to getting sexually sober attest that much of their prior therapy was taken up with the drama surrounding their sexual acting-out rather than the underlying painful concerns of their past histories. Only by first stopping their addictive sexual activities were they able to make full use of the therapeutic process and begin to grow out of the unhealthy coping behaviors they had begun to acquire early in their lives.

Looking Back

People have dramatically different responses to the prospect of investigating their early childhood problems. Most adults who were abused as children tend to idealize their childhoods. Even when they're recalling difficult or hurtful events, some adult survivors of childhood abuse describe their experience as "not especially bad." Others have no recollection of long periods of their childhood.

Even when a childhood history of direct trauma or abuse is painfully obvious, it can take a great deal of patience, support, and care for survivors to fully understand the emotional impact such experiences have caused and integrate this understanding into adult coping strategies. Often, early in treatment or therapy, people expect that they will remember or understand some single "event" or "truth" in their personal history and that the insight alone will cure or fix them. Unfortunately, it is highly unlikely that realizing any single truth will cure a lifetime of sex addiction and intimacy problems. It is important to take care in examining present experience and to go slow in looking at the past to make certain that the anxiety and feelings that are sure to arise over the course of therapy don't invite a return to sexual acting-out.

Below is a list of the kinds of childhood trauma that over time can contribute to sexually addictive patterns of behavior as those exposed to them mature into adults.

CHILDHOOD ABUSE CONCERNS

Physical: Being hit, beaten, spanked, whipped, abandoned, locked up alone for long periods, watching others be hit or beaten, excessive unwanted tickling.

Sexual Abuse *Overt*: Children under the age of 16 persuaded to engage in oral sex, genital sex acts, sexual touch, or masturbation with adults over the age of 18. Sexual stimulation by adults. Being asked to exhibit yourself, being exhibited to, deliberate exposure to porn by adults, deliberate exposure to sex by older children.

Sexual Abuse *Covert*: Exposure to sexual content in childhood (excessive nudity, sexual acts). Ending up as a surrogate emotional spouse to a troubled, alcoholic, or mentally ill mother or father. Seeing adult sex in the home, excessive talk about sex or genitalia, having your sexual development discussed in front of the family. Sex described as bad or dirty or never discussed at all.

Emotional Abuse: Being yelled at, devalued, subject to constant sarcasm, mind games, being the butt of jokes, being picked on, or threatened. Having your movements, creativity, ideas, or diet constantly monitored or controlled. Having to take sides in your parent's marital problems.

Intimidation: Constant fighting in the house, things getting thrown around or broken, doors slammed. Feeling that the house is not a safe place. Adult caregivers are absent or inconsistent, violent or threatening, unloving, or angry all the time. Being left alone to wait for punishment.

Physical Neglect: Inconsistent food or money sources; inconsistent shelter; constantly changing schools, families, and neighborhoods; unclean home or clothes. Being left alone for long periods of time with no activities, no structure. Lack of structure in the home—everyone fends for themselves. Made to take care of yourself at too young an age. No meals together, no cohesion among family members.

Emotional Neglect: Significant events which happen in the home or family are not discussed or celebrated, sex is not discussed, minimal physical contact, no hugs, consistently having to put the needs of an emotionally or physically troubled parent or sibling first, childhood consisting of all work and no playtime. Frequently let down, learning that caregivers promise things that are either taken away or forgotten about. Learning that you can't trust or rely on adults.

Homophobia: Told to "act like a man," forced to dress, act, or play in a more "masculine" way, called "sissy" or "fag" or "queer." Pushed around, beaten up, socially ignored, or laughed at; unwelcome in peer groups. Unable to talk about social abuses at home.

It's important to understand that abuse and neglect in and of themselves do not cause addictions. Addictions are, in part, maladaptations or unhealthy coping mechanisms learned in response to abuse and neglect. Addicts of all kinds have histories of abuse, but not everyone who has a history of neglect or abuse becomes an addict. Some people translate their painful early experiences into the creation of intense art, for example, or into lives devoted to selfless acts of giving. In short, a history of childhood sexual abuse or neglect does not guarantee that someone will become a sex addict or sex offender, but having experienced that kind of abuse does increase the chance of later developing addictive life patterns.

SELF-CONCEPTS

Children generally take a lot of responsibility for both the good and bad things that happen around them. People who grow up in families where relationships form around patterns of abuse, homophobia, or neglect—either emotional or physical—consciously and unconsciously assign themselves the blame for those negative experiences and usually carry negative feelings about themselves into adulthood.

These feelings are experienced as shame, low self-esteem, and a sense of unworthiness. The greater and earlier the experience of childhood abuse or neglect, the more intensely felt is the core of shame within.

These negative inner feelings of shame and self-loathing are key factors that drive addiction.[1] Here are some examples of these negative beliefs or self-concepts.

Self-Esteem

Belief: I am basically a bad and unworthy individual.

Thoughts that support this belief:
No matter what you see on the outside, underneath I am worthless. My sexual acting-out con-
firms my worthlessness. I am hopeless about ever
feeling healthy or normal. I feel like I have to work
harder than others just to look okay. I make many
mistakes but I can't ask for help and I can't show
my vulnerability because then you would see how
truly flawed I am.

Behaviors that support this belief:
Self-defeating or degrading life experiences are
often covered with a veneer of grandiosity, self-
righteous anger, or arrogance. Or they often manifest in underemployment, financial problems,
isolated or unhealthy living environments, or poor
self-care. Other such behaviors include refusing
to let anyone in emotionally to truly help, egocen-
tric and self-centered decision-making, sending
mixed messages, and bringing people into your life
but then pushing them away.

Body Image
Belief: I am unlovable as I am.

Thoughts that support this belief:
My body is not sexy or thin or muscular enough,
I am not attractive enough to get anyone to want
or love me. Look at how wonderful those other
men look! I will never look as good as they do. I
can't ever really show who I am inside because
once they really get to know me people will abandon me. Feelings and relationships are uncom-

fortable; it is better to keep my focus on the outside. If I only had more money, clothes, or success I would be okay.

Behaviors that support this belief:
Focus on body image, money, constant exercise or dieting, steroid use, body enhancements, overspending on clothes, trainers, etc. Always looking for the better looking guy to date or have sex with. Focusing on the external, exaggerating stories and experiences, trying to impress people to win them over. Always yearning for a bigger job, house, or car. Constantly comparing yourself to others and thinking that if you had what others have or do what others are doing, then you will be happy and others will want and desire you.

Some men with these issues consistently allow men whom they deem "hotter" than themselves to use them sexually in order to feel worthwhile.

Relationships

Belief #1: My needs are never going to be met if I have to depend on someone else.
Belief #2: If you really get close to me you won't love me or you will leave me.

Thoughts that support this belief:
Only through luck or careful strategy can I achieve happiness. I have to seduce someone to get them to want or love me. Even if I find someone, eventually I will be abandoned. I want someone because I don't want to be alone, but I can't let anyone get too close to me because then I will get hurt.

Behaviors that support this belief:
Lying, keeping secrets, living a double life, lovers on the side, leading a driven, intense, controlled life. Being busy all the time, workaholism, constantly taking care of other people's needs, recreational activities that are limited to acting out with intensity. Manipulating relationships to keep others from leaving. Ambivalent and noncommittal about relationship intentions. Affecting the appearance of being unaffected by external issues or problems—cultivating a demeanor of detachment. Seeking relationships with unavailable partners, looking for and longing for straight guys. Lacking personal warmth or emotional availability to others (and subsequently confused and hurt when those others aren't closer and more intimate).

Sexuality
Belief: Nothing is more important to me than sex.

Thoughts that support this belief:
I want all the hot guys I can get. Why pass up a good opportunity to have sex? Having a lot of sex is part of being gay. People who don't have sex whenever they can are just boring and not hip. Monogamy is a heterosexual concept. Being with men means having as much sex as you want.

Behaviors that support this belief:
Opportunities for sexual activity are seized wherever possible—behavior that borders on exploitative or predatory. Few boundaries are maintained

between friendships and lovers. Any time is a good time for some kind of seduction and sex. Drugs are often involved. The physical self is defined by what will attract others, by what will turn heads. Nonsexual situations like work or time with friends are "tolerated" until free to go cruise for sex. Self-worth is defined by the frequency of sexual encounters, but the sex actually feels emptier and emptier over time. Friendships are often shallow and superficial or defined by sex.

HOMOPHOBIA AND SHAME

Shame is a core emotion underlying and driving much addictive behavior. Gay sex addicts have multiple layers of shame in addition to those we might expect in someone who grew up in an abusive, dysfunctional, or neglectful family.

Gay children experience shame and stigma because they often have to hide homosexual feelings that are unacceptable to their peers and families. Even if they don't identify or understand their "gayness" at an early age, most homosexual and bisexual men speak of having felt "different" or "knowing they were different from other boys," some as early as 4 or 5 years old. As a result, most gay children and adolescents learn to hide the parts of themselves that they know will not be acceptable or rewarded and will likely be devalued.

Many men remember worrying that their peers teased them if they exhibited traits that were "less masculine." First in the family and later in the social surroundings of school and peer play, males learn that it is risky or even dangerous to openly demonstrate interests or behaviors that lie outside patterns of "typical" male behavior. Graeme Hanson and Lawrence Hartmann, in their groundbreaking research on male homosexuality, describe this experience of isolation:

Boys called "sissies" often have few ways to express their distress about being different and about being teased. Some respond to social pressure by increasing gender-conforming behavior (thereby hiding parts of themselves). Others respond with shame, lower self-esteem, depression, and a diminished ability to interact with, enjoy, and learn from peers (isolation). Not infrequently, the people to whom such boys would turn for adult support and comfort—their parents—are also uncomfortable with and lack understanding of the child's experience of being different. These effects can be carried forward into adulthood as a lifelong view of interpersonal relationships consisting of some kind of wariness or distrust of self or others that the young man will bring into future relationships.[2]

This "distrust or wariness of self or others" that Hanson and Hartmann speak of is a symptom of shame. In order to protect themselves from hurt or embarrassment, many gay children learn to hide or reject the parts of themselves that others might find objectionable. It is hard to learn trust and intimacy when you feel you have to hide parts of yourself in order to feel safe and survive.

The gay adolescent can't help taking in the negative names and messages his peers use to describe boys who are attracted to other boys (faggot, sissy, queer) when he suspects that he himself is or may be such a boy. This type of conflict produces shame about what he is and shame around sex and his sexual feelings.

This specific type of shame—the fear of discovery and/or rejection for being homosexual—is at the root of internalized homophobia, which influences the later development of self-esteem, self-worth, and the ability to be intimate and genuine with others. The pressure of growing up feeling different in an unacceptable way and having to learn to hide that difference is an emotional stressor with which most heterosexual children do not have to contend. This, in part, accounts for the higher levels of multiple addictions and emotional problems that we see among adult gay men. Children of other minority groups often also experience this kind of stress, and its negative influence on adult emotional life, self-esteem, and social relationships is well-documented.

GAY SURVIVAL

In sum, nearly every gay child learns to hide parts of himself to "fit in," which reduces his opportunities for genuine social and family interaction. This emotional isolation, coupled with the fear of being "found out," amplifies the experiences and behaviors that contribute to addiction. Juan, a 29-year-old Latino, relates how years of internalized homophobia contributed to his double life as a sex addict and nearly destroyed his five-year relationship:

> I finally got help after Jeremy came home early one day and found me in our house—in our bed—having unprotected sex with a male prostitute. At first I said that this had never happened before, that I had always been faithful, but Jeremy just didn't buy that. He told me he would leave me for sure if I didn't tell him the truth. I finally told him that I have been with a lot of guys on and off, casually, throughout our relationship, despite the fact that we had promised to be monogamous.

Juan later revealed that his sexual escapades were part of an even longer-term pattern of both anonymous sex and keeping sexual secrets:

> Growing up, I certainly knew better than to talk to anyone about being gay, and being gay to me meant having sex with men. My parents would have thrown me out of the family if they had known, and the church said what I was doing meant I was going to hell—sex with men was a sin.
>
> There was no one to talk to where I grew up; even though I was really sexually active from the minute I hit adolescence. I had this total double life, looking like a Catholic choirboy on the outside and then having sex with what seemed like half the boys in the neighborhood behind closed doors.
>
> Even though I never felt like I could be loved, valued, or even attractive in my family life, I always felt desired and important when guys would want me for sex. As I got older, it seemed natural to continue to keep my sexual life to myself; I figured it wasn't anybody's business.
>
> When I met Jeremy and fell in love, I wanted to tell him that I didn't know how not to be with other guys and that monogamy seemed impossible to me. But it just seemed so important to him, and in the beginning it wasn't all that hard to do because we were in love and I didn't really even want anyone else. But then, as time went on, I started cruising again and then secretly started having casual sex with other guys. It just was impossible for me to admit the truth. I had no idea how to even start talking about it

and just felt sure that he would leave me if he knew.

Juan's story illustrates how the secret sexual "double life" he developed during childhood had shaped his adult relationship with Jeremy. Though Juan had escaped the early repressive environments of church and family, Jeremy's request for commitment and monogamy left Juan feeling trapped in an emotional dilemma similar to that of his childhood.

Having never dealt with his addictive sexual behavior patterns and lacking the skills either to reach out for help or trust his partner by being honest, Juan returned to his adolescent pattern of hiding or splitting off parts of himself and his sexual behavior. And as before, he felt ashamed and isolated from those closest to him. Eventually, the conflict between his two worlds brought about a crisis that nearly lost him his relationship.

HOMOPHOBIA, SHAME, AND ADDICTION

The shame gay sex addicts feel is often directly related to their compulsive patterns of sexual behavior. In fact there is double shame for the gay sex addict; no matter how much he may have worked through his negative feelings about being gay, he still ends up feeling ashamed of his sexual acting-out. This double shame reinforces the impulse toward a secret sexual life. We can see this tendency in Steven's story:

> During college I would hit all of the restrooms on campus for sex. Whenever I had a final or the pressure was on, there I was cruising behind closed doors and peeking under stalls looking for sex. I found a lot of older guys looking for college-age kids, but also young guys like me who mostly just seemed ashamed of what they were doing and ran out of there as soon as it was over. When I would see one of them on campus, we would

always pretend like we had never met.

Back then I thought I was straight, that I just went to bathrooms for sex to relieve stress. I was still dating a girl and even thought about getting married. But even after college, when I was still living with my girlfriend, I used to cruise adult bookstores for hours, having sex with men on my lunch hour or before I went home at night.

When we broke up and I finally came out as a gay man, I figured that once I settled down with a guy and got into a same-sex relationship I wouldn't want to go looking for anonymous sex anymore. Finally, I wouldn't have to keep my sex life a secret! I blamed my habits of cruising the parks, malls, and school tearooms on my having been so closeted. What a shock to find that once I was no longer living with a woman and didn't have anyone to come home to, my cruising activity tripled! Then, instead of focusing on finding the right guy— which is what I said I really wanted to do—I found myself spending two to three hours a day in saunas and parks, having sex with strangers.

It took getting arrested for masturbating in an adult theater for me to begin to see that I really did have a problem and that the problem had nothing to do with trying to be straight or unhappiness about being gay. It was something else entirely.

THE POWER OF INSIGHT—THE HELPFUL PART

Understanding that sex addicts act out in an attempt to meet deeper emotional problems helps to eliminate the stigma society places on sex addiction and helps to reduce some of the shame gay sex addicts feel about their behavior. At their core, sex addicts feel defective, broken, or deeply flawed. Although these feelings are reinforced by the sexual behaviors themselves, most sex addicts have had underlying negative feelings about themselves for most of their lives.

While many sex addicts affect an outward arrogance, pride, or grandiosity about their sexual prowess and adventures, this posturing is usually a mask that hides deeper feelings of low self-esteem and self-hatred. Coming to terms with the fact that your addictive behaviors developed as a means of emotional survival—not because deep down you are a bad, disloyal, or defective individual—can go a long way toward reducing your underlying feelings of paralyzing shame and self-hatred.

Men who act out sexually are not sleazy, untrustworthy, or uncaring—although their actions and behaviors may fit these descriptions at times. It's closer to the truth to say that sex addicts find it difficult to sustain feelings of self-love and validation through the safe, consistent support of friends and lovers. Addicts are destined to repeat the quest for love and admiration through sex and romantic intensity until they get the direction and support they need to stop their sexually compulsive acting-out. Once they stop, they can begin to examine and heal the pain that underlies their addiction and move on to healthier forms of genuine intimacy and connection.

THE POWER OF INSIGHT— THE LESS HELPFUL PART

The big book of Alcoholics Anonymous helpfully states, "Insight alone availed us nothing."

Although there is great value in understanding that physiological and psychological problems underlie most addictions, simply having this understanding doesn't provide a cure! This is the problem with trying to utilize traditional psychotherapy to eliminate addictions. Understanding and insight may reduce shame and offer some direction toward change, but ultimately they won't resolve an active addiction.

Managing an addiction is no different from dealing with any chronic medical problem where getting an accurate diagnosis is only the first step toward healing and recovery. If by reading this or working with a professional you have come to believe that sex addiction is a problem for you, then you must then take active steps toward solving it.

SEEKING THE CURE

Many people who read books like this one, enter 12-step programs, seek therapy, and check into treatment centers are seeking "the answer." They want to solve all their problems and answer all their questions—as if their addiction were an equation in a math quiz.

Some will drop out or give up when they find out that they aren't going to be cured once they "figure it out." The problem is that they don't actually want or know how to work to solve the problem; somehow they think that having that "Ah-ha" moment of understanding will be enough.

No amount of information is going to stop a sex addict from repeating patterns of problem behavior. You can only meaningfully change your behavior by taking deliberate, ongoing, active, and committed steps toward change. While this and previous chapters have described and discussed understanding sexual addiction, upcoming chapters will focus on creating change. As we move forward, we'll learn how to make this happen one day at a time. But first, let's consider how party drugs and other addictive substances become intertwined with sex addiction.

CHAPTER 4
CRYSTAL, SEX, AND OTHER ADDICTIONS

Here's a story from Philip, 29 years old, seeking help for the first time:

> Half the guys I meet online end up offering me Tina. We usually spend the weekend watching porn or having sex with other men who show up. If I am too high to get it up or keep it up, I always keep Viagra or Cialis around, or I can get it shipped out overnight via the Internet. Out at the bars there is a constant supply of Special K, GHB, or X. When I do that, I end up in the sex clubs till after the sun comes up. I wouldn't know where to begin dealing with how I have sex since the whole problem feels so tied together with my partying and my social life and always has.

Many addicts struggle with multiple addictions—having more than one substance and/or behavioral addiction operating at the same time. According to a survey of male sex addicts, both straight and gay, approximately 87% of respondents reported more than one addictive substance use or behavior in their histories.[1] Though more research is needed, it's reasonable to think that gay male sex addicts would tend to report a higher frequency of multiple addictions than their straight counter-parts, since gay men have higher substance abuse rates than straight men. Some data suggest the incidence of drug and alcohol abuse in gay men is as high as 30% (similar data report that 10% to 12% of the general population abuses addictive substances).[2]

Theories abound about why there is a greater rate of drug and alcohol addiction among gays, and the source of the problem is biological, familial, environmental, or cultural, depending on the bias of the theorist. Most likely, some combination of these factors contributes to the patterns of addiction among gay men. One noted researcher wrote: "The use of substances can be associated with ... coming out and self-acceptance for many gay men ... while internalized and societal homophobia combine to reinforce the use of alcohol and drugs."[3]

CULTURAL REINFORCEMENT FOR ADDICTION

Though urban gay men today have a greater array of social and recreational activities available to them than ever before—including volunteer and recreational groups, dating and parenting clubs, and supportive professional and spiritual organizations—for many men in the urban gay community, public social activity remains tied to settings that either reinforce the use of alcohol, drugs, the drive toward achieving the perfect body, or the pursuit of sex and romance. It is no coincidence that many of the most consistently successful private local businesses in the gay community remain the bars, the gyms, the party circuit, and the bathhouses and sex clubs. Many popular gay publications would not survive without the glut of advertising promoting physical perfection, sexual massage, prostitution, and sexual partnering or romance.

This state of affairs reinforces the association in the gay community between sex, romance, body enhancement, and easy access to mind-altering chemicals, which means that men who are already struggling for a stable sense of physical and emotional self-worth must confront the prospect of multiple addictions. Taken together, the circuit parties, cruisy gay gyms, the bar-club scene, and even the bathhouses can be vibrant, healthily integrated dimensions of a gay man's life. They also have a darker side, which challenges men with limited emotional resources and intimacy skills and exposes them to behaviors that they are ill-equipped to handle. Rather than liberating these men, the social scenes in many urban gay communities imprison them in repetitive patterns of drug use and sexual acting-out

HIV, AGING, AND DRUGS

In response to HIV and AIDS, many gay men—both old and young—use drugs and sex to simply check out. Many mature gay men, positive and negative, survived the AIDS-ravaged 1980s and early 1990s but lost many or all of the gay friends and lovers of their youth. Faced with this immeasurable hurt and forced to develop new social circles and sexual networks, some of these men turn to quick online or phone sex hookups that, combined with disinhibiting party drugs like crystal meth, can temporarily recreate a lost sense of empowerment, desirability, and youth. The advent of phone sex and the Internet has provided almost instant access to both drugs and sex. Street drugs—particularly crystal—are the great equalizers for older gay men. If they feel physically inferior or less desirable than a younger, "more perfect specimen," they can completely lose these anxieties and fears after just a line or two. One addict had this to say about his crystal use:

> In the '80s, when all my friends were alive, it was always, you know, the gang getting together for the

dinner, the gang doing this or that. But then they all died. I'm a long-term survivor with HIV. I'm here and they're not. So my weekends can be very, very lonely. And as a result of that, my drug usage has increased.[4]

Some HIV-positive addicts relate that learning about their diagnosis became the catalyst for a long period of sexual acting-out and drug use. Another man with these feelings describes his experience this way:

I just didn't care anymore. I tried to be safe and when I got it, I was, like, "fuck it." And I don't care who gets hurt now. I started having sex and using [crystal] with a vengeance. I hit the sex clubs all weekend, every weekend and I was tweaking like there was no tomorrow. As far as I was concerned, there *was* no tomorrow. Looking back now I feel a lot of shame about the men I might have infected—but at the time the unspoken rule was "don't ask and don't tell." I was so filled with anger, hurt, and resentment that I think I just wanted to fuck it out of me.

For some younger gay men—bridling against the "safe sex" messages drilled into them everywhere and the endless associations between sex, testing, illness, and death—easily obtainable party drugs, fast sex online, phone sex, and casual hookups can temporarily banish the specter of mortality. These men just want to "have fun!"

Many of them will find that this intensity-based party period of their lives will wane over time, eventually to be replaced with more meaningful intimacies and priorities. But as in any situation where addictive substances and behaviors are involved, some men will become increasingly addicted to the combination of drugs and intense sexual experiences and find it difficult to move beyond this way of life, even if they want to.

Over the past two decades, gay communities have been decimated by AIDS. The impact of HIV continues to directly influence the sexual lives of millions of Americans—and gay men in particular. Crystal users have described the drug as a way to dissociate from the fear and responsibility now inextricably associated with sex as a consequence of AIDS.[5]

For some men, the timing of crystal's appearance on the gay scene is perfect. The drug quells feelings of hopelessness and low self-esteem and fits neatly into habits and institutions already present in many devastated gay communities.

ABOUT CRYSTAL

Methamphetamine is by far the most dangerous and troublesome drug to have infiltrated the gay community. Often called "the sex drug," crystal meth is the "party favor" of choice for anonymous sexual activity in bathhouses and sex clubs and on the Internet. Like all amphetamines (speed), crystal meth lends the user feelings of intensity, power, and drive to whatever activity the user engages in. If cleaning houses while you're high on crystal is your thing, then while you're high you're a compulsive house-cleaner, up all night, feeling fabulous, energized, and creative with every swish of the sponge—at least until you start coming down. Similarly, users say the drug allows them to keep being sexual for an entire day—even two or three—at a time without coming down, sleeping, or eating. Safe sex is often not a high priority for drug-addicted men who have grown accustomed to having multiple anonymous partners, for dozens of hours at a time. One recovering drug and sex addict reports, "When I do crystal meth, the sex just goes on forever." Another states, "There's no love, no caring, no emotion involved. I don't even care who they are, or even what their names are."

Methamphetamine—known on the street as crystal, crank, tweak, Tina, tweedy, go-fast, and dozens of other names—is also sold legally in tablet form as the prescription drug Dioxin. More often, though, it's cooked in makeshift labs and sold on the street as a powder, which is injected, snorted, or swallowed. The smokable form of crystal is called "ice" and looks like tiny pieces of rock candy. Widely available in the 1960s, crystal faded in the 1970s as controls were tightened on legal production, and cocaine took its place as the new party drug of choice. Crack cocaine dominated the 1980s along with designer drugs like Ecstasy, but in the early 1990s, crystal made a comeback and seems here to stay.

Like other kinds of speed, meth directly affects the user's brain and spinal cord by interfering with neurotransmitters, which are naturally produced by nerve cells to aid in intercellular communication. Meth most directly affects the neurotransmitter dopamine, which helps to regulate how good we feel about ourselves. By manipulating their dopamine levels with meth, users say they get a unique, clean high that can't be duplicated by other drugs.

The mental health director of a major GLBT community services center offered these thoughts on her meth-addicted clients:

> Once you've experienced that mood state, you just want to have it again and again. Unfortunately, when you come down—after there's been such a stimulation of the brain chemicals that regulate your mood when you're using crystal—you are

amazingly depressed, which of course is part of the addictive cycle.

We have a lot of weekend users. They'll use for maybe 48 hours of the weekend, go to work feeling like hell on a Monday, not really feel good again until Wednesday or Thursday, and do it again on weekends. But a drug so powerful can definitely have permanent side effects. In terms of [the] long-term effects, it actually changes your brain chemistry, It stimulates your neurotransmitters that cause you to be in a good mood, but then unfortunately when you stop using the meth your body has to replenish those neurotransmitters, and that's hard to do. So after consistent use of methamphetamine, you've actually changed your brain chemistry, and it can take up to two years of not using to recover, depending on your habit.

I have one client—a 10-year user—who's now been off for about a year, but he still has unbelievable cravings. Because that's part of it too—it's the ritual. There's a rush and addiction with the ritual with the way you use, and then you pair it with the sex, which is a tremendous reinforcer.[6]

In a recent article in *Frontiers* magazine, Steve, a successful white-collar professional, talked about how crystal differed from other drugs he had used:

I always partied, and no matter what I did—coke, X, alcohol—I always remained in control. I had even done crystal meth a few times (I once got high in a Port-o-Potty at Long Beach Pride with my roommate in the mid '90s). But no matter how much I played, I kept my drug use purely recreational. Last year, though, as my relationship with my live-in boyfriend was ending, I started using meth on a regular basis. I had a dealer friend, and it was totally an escape from reality. Jack—my boyfriend—and I had stopped having sex, and we both knew it was only a matter of time before we broke up. Lonely and eager to use sex with other guys as a weapon, I started going online for anonymous encounters. The drug was everywhere, and I quickly learned that "PnP"—the ubiquitous code on sex sites for "Party and Play"—actually meant drinking Gatorade and smoking meth. That's all anybody was doing.

Like so many gay men, Steve found the drug made him want to have sex—a lot of it—with anyone else who was on the drug. Meth completely distorted Steve's perspective on time:

Six or eight hours would go by, and it felt like five minutes. You have no focus on time. Even when I would say "I'm going home now," another three hours would go by. I always topped and never performed oral sex. In my mind, they were servicing me; those were the precautions in my head. And let me tell you, no one was using a condom.

Steve noted that while he was on meth he often had sex with men he otherwise would never have considered sleeping with. Because meth was cheap and easy to get, Steve never once bought the drug, since his Internet hookups were always willing to supply him with it for free.

To counteract "crystal dick" (drug-induced impotence), Steve said that everyone was taking Viagra to maintain their erections. Some of the bottoms used a syringe to inject meth in their anuses for a "booty bump," which allowed them to perform without any pain for hours. Many of his sex partners offered Steve sleeping pills to help him come off the high, since the drug sometimes kept him up for days even after the fun began to wear off. Soon the need for meth started to creep up on him, and he started using it to get to work every morning.

> Most of my friends and coworkers had no idea I had a problem, but there were little signs that something was wrong. I started calling in sick. The drug was causing paranoia when I would come down, and I found myself obsessively picking the skin on my arms, making myself bleed, which left little scrapes and scabs from my wrists to my elbows. I had no idea how much it started to take hold. It's scary how it creeps up on you. I look back and wonder, "What the hell was I thinking and doing?" Despite this I just couldn't drop meth the way I had set aside other drugs. Although there was no physical withdrawal, as with heroin or coke, the drug still had a powerful pull that I couldn't get away from. I would go three or four weeks and be fine, then this little voice inside me would plant the seed and I would be back out there sexing and using.

Effective treatment for multiple addictions that fuse drug use and sexual activity must address not only the substance use but also the addictive, intensity-based nature of anonymous sex.

People who use crystal and other forms of speed whenever they are having a lot of sex report having a very difficult time returning to patterns of sexuality or intimacy that are not related to drug use. Recovery from these kinds of addictive interactions requires a long-term reintroduction of human relatedness into sex to help reestablish ties to intimacy and relational sexuality. Many meth abusers have not had anything other than a casual or anonymous sexual experience in many years.

MULTIPLE ADDICTION PATTERNS

The use of drugs and alcohol can reinforce addictive sexual behavior and merge with sexuality itself in the experience of the user. Following are some of the ways that substance abuse and sexual behavior become intertwined:

Escalation: Using drugs in conjunction with sex can increase the type or frequency of your sexual activities. "I was never into multiple partners until I started snorting crystal and drinking. Then, after a while, I just didn't care who or how many guys did me. I also used to be really careful about what I put inside me, but now if I get high enough, I just want it big and I want it rough."

Fusion: Drug use and sex become fused so that sex is no longer interesting or fun unless drugs are a key part of the experience. One user says, "No sex compares to sex when you're doing crystal. I don't even bother having straight sex anymore. I tried a few times, but I don't even get it up; it's boring. Now I just wait till the weekend when I can do some bumps. Then I start looking online to hook up."

Linking: Drug use and sex are linked in patterns of behavior. In other words, you become accustomed to getting high in certain ways as a part of your sexual rituals. These patterns then become the norm. "When it comes to hooking up with other guys I never go out unless I am pretty high. I drink at home until I feel ready, smoke some dope, then I go out to the bar to try to meet somebody. But I don't get high if I am just masturbating to porn; I do that just to get off."

Switching: Going from the use of one substance or behavior to another in an attempt to eliminate a different problem behavior. For example, Frank tried to deal with his compulsive use of male prostitutes by attending 12-step support groups, and his sexual acting-out stopped. However, he soon began gaining significant amounts of weight, which continued over the first six months of his recovery. Never having learned to manage the emotional stress underlying his addictive behavior, he had switched the addictive use of sexual activity for compulsive eating. Unrecovered alcoholics and drug addicts will frequently switch one substance for another, blaming the specific drug or type of alcohol for the problem instead of dealing with their substance use as part of a larger problem.

Bingeing/Purging: The attempt to deal with sex or other addictive problems by swearing off the behavior altogether. After his second lewd-conduct arrest in a public park, Jorge convinced himself that his problem was having given in to having sex with men and having turned away from his church. He wasn't able to distinguish his sex addiction problem from his homosexuality. In pain and feeling shame after being arrested and continually seeking sex with strangers (which went against his beliefs), he decided that he would eliminate sex with men from his life (purging) and embrace an intensely devout religious practice (thereby switching addictions). This "cure" lasted only a few weeks. At first Jorge had feelings of euphoria and relief; he felt he had solved his problem. Then, after a stressful workday, he went out drinking and the dam burst. Within a few hours he was right back at the same park where he had been arrested twice before.

WHERE TO BEGIN: SUBSTANCES OR BEHAVIORS?

Drug and alcohol addictions are critical problems which nearly always have to be eliminated first before the issues underlying behavioral and fantasy-based addictions such as sex can be addressed. Drugs and alcohol are disinhibiting—they weaken your judgment to the point where you cannot remain committed to other boundaries you may have previously set for yourself (like not having certain kinds of sex). Unless the man abusing drugs and alcohol gets sober, it is unlikely that he will be able to change his sexual behavior for very long.

Some exceptions to the rule of "getting sober first" apply to addicts who have so fused drug and sex addiction that they cannot remain sober because of their sexual acting-out. These addicts need to address their substance use and sexual acting-out *at the same time* in order to stay sober on either front!

Some lifelong patterns of drug and alcohol abuse mask underlying emotional concerns, which are difficult if not impossible to understand until the user stops using. Steven recounts his story:

> I guess, looking back, it sounds funny, but I never really knew that I was an alcoholic or drug addict. I mean I drank almost every night, but usually just wine, like with dinner, you know. That made it easier to deny. And then of course there were the martinis—apple, chocolate, whatever flavor was on at the bar, I mean everyone was drinking those;

I just seemed to have a few more than everyone else did—and of course whatever drugs were around to go with the drinking—but it always seemed manageable.

But over time there just seemed to be too many ugly mornings after when I'd wake up with guys I didn't know and didn't want to know. Too many days having to face the morning sun after a weekend in a sex club, the multiple times my wallet was stolen, and all the angry fights with friends and lovers who eventually withdrew from me. Not to mention the times I had to figure out exactly where my car was.

It just never occurred to me that I might have a problem with alcohol or drugs. Even though I spent some time in counseling and therapy, no one really suggested that I should stop drinking or using. It wasn't until I tried to change my sexual behavior—then there it was, right in my face, because I couldn't stop acting out sexually. As hard as I tried, as many promises as I made to myself—to start dating or to get to know the guys I was having sex with—as soon as I would have a few drinks or get high, I was right where I started. I couldn't stop hitting on guys in bars, cruising the Internet for sex, or heading back out to the bathhouse.

When I got sober I started to realize that I had never really felt comfortable hooking up with men unless I was high in some way—that without the substances to bolster me I often felt shy, uncertain, and withdrawn. I certainly didn't like sex as much sober. It seems that most of my adult life I had only gotten off with men when I was loaded. That was when I felt most comfortable having sex.

Steven was one year into his Alcoholics Anonymous recovery when he wrote the paragraphs above. His longstanding problems with sex and relationships forced him to come to grips with his substance addictions. His sexual acting-out ended only after he got chemically sober. He will, however, need to keep a watchful eye over his future sexual activities, since going to the wrong place or person for sex could lead him back to drugs and alcohol.

ADDRESSING MULTIPLE ADDICTIONS

Clearly, some sex addicts have related concerns that have to be tackled at the same time, if they want to halt their obsessive and addictive patterns of sexual acting-out. Consider the man who is trying to get sober from cocaine abuse but is also addicted to seeing prostitutes. Perhaps for a time he is successful at refraining from smoking crack, only to relapse when the prostitutes he hires are either using drugs or seeking them. We see a similar plight in the experience of an addict trying to escape a crystal meth problem who continues to have anonymous sex in bathhouses and sex clubs. How can he stay sober when he goes to those places for sex and men offer him crystal or Ecstasy?

Men who identify with these issues may need to address both drug use and sexual choices simultaneously for recovery to take place. This means the multiply addicted man has to do more than simply stop using a substance. If he is serious about change, he will have to get help changing his sexual habits and many of his daily patterns of behavior—perhaps even distancing himself from people who may encourage or indulge his addictions.

All addictions fall into two fairly distinct categories: substance addictions or behavioral addictions. Here's a brief list.

Substance Addictions
- Alcohol
- Drugs
- Food
- Cigarettes (Nicotine)

Behavioral Addictions
- Gambling
- Sex
- Work
- Exercise
- Spending
- Religion

Drugs can be divided into three categories:

Street Drugs
Crystal meth, Ecstasy, Special K (ketamine), GHB, LSD, marijuana, heroin, etc.

Prescription Drugs
Sleeping pills (Ambien, Seconal)
Pain medications (Vicodin, OxyContin)
Steroids
Amphetamines (Dexedrine, Benzedrine, methedrine)
Mild tranquilizers (Xanax, Valium, Ativan)
Diet pills (Phentermine, etc.)

Over-the-counter Drugs
Benadryl
Sleeping aids
Cough and cold solutions
Pseudoephedrine

It can be difficult to differentiate between recreational drug use and addiction. Below, you'll find the signs and characteristics common to all addictions that doctors and addiction specialists use to diagnose addiction. This list may be useful in determining whether more than one problem lurks in a complex pattern of addictive behavior. Some of these characteristics of addiction will be familiar from earlier chapters; they are included here specifically to support an examination of multiple addictions.[7]

1. Addictions tend to *escalate* in several ways:
   a) Increasing amounts of the potentially addicting substance or behavior(s) are used.
   b) More time is involved in the using.
   c) More effort is devoted to obtaining or getting to the substance or activity.

2. Addictions tend to have *serious consequences*— which are usually minimized or denied by the user—in multiple life areas such as work, relationships, health, and finances.

3. Addicts often have a history of *failed attempts to control* the amount of their using, the amount of time they devote to their using, or the type of substance or behavior they use.

4. The use of the substance or behavior is *carried out in secret*, or only the user knows the actual degree of his use or activity.

5. Addictions are often accompanied by underlying *feelings of shame*, which are exposed if the user's behavior is discovered.

6. Addiction to substances or behaviors often results in a *failure to fulfill major obligations* at work, school, or home (repeated absences or poor work performance related to substance use or sexual activity or both; neglect of primary relationship or family).

7. Addictions get acted out in situations that *put the user and/or others in physical danger* (driving a car when impaired or risking HIV transmission).

HOMEWORK: TEST YOURSELF

One tried and true way to determine whether you're addicted to a behavior or substance is simply to take some time away from it. A written commitment to limit or eliminate the use of a substance or problem activity for at least 30 days will provide good insight into what function this activity actually serves in your life and whether your relationship to it is addictive (or just characteristic of a bad habit).

Many addicts prevent themselves from getting well by switching from one problematic substance or experience to another without observing their recurring pattern of behavior as they cycle through several addictive rituals. With this in mind, make careful note of any new or unusual patterns of behavior that pop up during your 30-day time-out.

Another way to break through denial around addiction issues is to share your concerns about your drug use, partying, spending, eating, or other behaviors with close friends or family who are not involved in these activities themselves. *Thoroughly* explaining the nature of your behaviors to someone who cares about you invites important, objective feedback from people who can see through your habits of denial and secrecy. This strategy affords you more support and vigilance in your recovery than if you were to simply try to make changes on your own.

Some people who need help with drug and alcohol addictions—or with severe problems such as bingeing/purging, compulsive exercise, and steroid abuse—may require the intervention of a medical professional. Others may require specialized support from fellow addicts in various 12-step programs (Alcoholics Anonymous, Crystal Meth Anonymous, Narcotics Anonymous, Overeaters Anonymous, Debtors Anonymous), the help of a professional therapist, or the structure of a more formal treatment program. We'll begin to take a closer look at the process of recovery from sex addiction in the next chapter.

CHAPTER 5
STARTING SEX ADDICTION RECOVERY: THE BOUNDARY PLAN

MY OWN THINKING IS THE PROBLEM

To the outsider it might seem a simple task to make permanent changes in your sexual behavior: "Just say no!" Stay away from certain places, stop hanging out with particular people, throw away certain magazines, videos, and online or club memberships. Learn new habits and get it together. Simple, right?

Well, the directions themselves seem fairly basic. But for sex addicts, the problem with following through on these simple ideas lies within the mind of the addict himself. Consider the words of Chris, who was addicted to cruising and hooking up for anonymous sex with men he met online:

> I made endless promises to change my behavior—
> promises to myself and promises to my lover.
> Always, over time my commitments and promises
> faded away until I was back doing the same stuff
> I started out doing in the first place. It was an end-
> less cycle. Without some kind of defined plan for
> change and accountability to someone else for
> that plan, I was like one of those caged hamsters

on a wheel, just going round and round but not getting anywhere.

Though he may be quite successful in making clear, life-affirming or success-oriented decisions in other areas of his life, a sex addict suffers from impaired thinking in the areas of romance and sexuality. Therefore the sex addict *cannot* solely rely on his judgment and decision-making in this area. On Monday, waking up in a good mood, he may be very determined to stop acting out, but by Wednesday, feeling stressed and uncomfortable, he may cross every sexual boundary he ever made for himself—and then some.

This is perhaps the most difficult challenge for any recovering individual: accepting that he can't make healthy decisions in one of the most deeply personal areas of his life. Addicts must follow a carefully defined written plan and—more importantly—make consistent use of helpful friends and acquaintances. The painful truth beneath these facts: Addicts cannot stay sexually sober by themselves.

MAKING A PLAN

The first step to take after you've determined that you have a sex addiction problem is to create a written plan of action that separates your addictive sexual behavior from healthy sex. This plan will help you define your *sexual sobriety*.

In order for recovery from any addiction to take place, there must be a clear bottom-line definition of the addict's sobriety. While the alcoholic or drug addict who has decided to get sober already has a concrete definition of sobriety—namely, eliminating his use of all mind-altering chemicals—sex addicts have a somewhat more challenging task ahead.

Happily, recovery from sex addiction *does not mean eliminating sex from your life*. Although it's often wise to take a short time-out from sexual activity in the early stages of recovery (see the remarks on celibacy below), the ultimate goal is to gain a sense of self-defined healthy sexuality—not to stop having sex altogether!

In this way recovery from sex and love addiction is more closely related to recovery from an eating disorder. Just as the former binge eater or bulimic must learn to integrate healthy eating into his or her life, so the sex addict must follow an individualized plan of healthy, life-affirming sexuality. This chapter is dedicated to the creation of such a plan toward healthy sexuality and intimacy for gay sex addicts.

Sober alcoholics use total abstention from alcohol and all mind-altering chemicals as their bottom-line sobriety definition. Their sobriety date is the day they first gave up using drugs and alcohol. Thus they have a clear start date from which to measure their length of sobriety.

Sexual sobriety, by contrast, is best defined by a contract, written up by and subject to agreement between the sex addict and someone in a 12-step-recovery support group: a sponsor, therapist, reliable friend, or clergyperson. These written sobriety contracts—or **Sexual Boundary Plans**—involve carefully defined, concrete behaviors from which the addict is committed to abstain.

Eli, a recovering sex addict, says:

> In my mind I always knew what was okay for me to do sexually and what was not okay, but somehow in the moment I seemed to end up changing the rules and ending up back where I started. It seemed like the sexual definitions in my head were always perfectly clear right up to the moment I ran into some hot guy that I couldn't resist. Then all the rules and agreements I had

made up in my head just went out the window. It wasn't until I actually wrote up a sexual boundary plan with the help of a close friend who understood my problem and then became accountable to that plan by checking in with him daily that I really began sticking to my commitments.

The plan also helped me bring into much clearer perspective the times and places where I am vulnerable to sexual acting-out no matter how many promises I make to myself that I won't. For example, I can remember telling myself that I wouldn't go have sex in the sex clubs, but that I would go there "just to see who was there" or "check out the scene." There wasn't a single time I told myself those things when I didn't end up having sex there anyway. Big surprise!

A written sexual boundary plan helped me to see that I was just lying to myself all along. Simply put, there are places and situations that I just cannot go and remain sexually sober. Writing it down and checking in with someone else has kept me from fooling myself when tempted.

THE SEXUAL BOUNDARY PLAN

You begin the process of defining your sexual sobriety by identifying those sexual or romantic activities that **cause shame**, that you **keep secret**, and any behaviors that are **illegal or abusive to others.**[1] All successful sexual recovery plans include clearly defined boundaries. Some men's plans are very simple written agreements: "No sexual or romantic activity of any kind outside my committed relationship" or "No sex in any public places or situations where I could ever be arrested."

Definitions of recovery often evolve over time as the sex addict's understanding of himself and his history deepens. One man's comparatively complex commitment may be: *"My sexual sobriety means I do not date anyone who is in a heterosexual marriage, in another relationship, anyone whom I would not introduce to friends, or anyone who is abusive or emotionally unresponsive to me."* A somewhat simpler plan states: *"I am sober as long as I do not pay for sex in any form."* The important points are simply to start somewhere, to be accountable to the plan, and to enlist the support of someone else.

WRITING A COMPREHENSIVE SEXUAL BOUNDARY PLAN

The underlying foundation of any boundaries that you set up around your sexual behavior must be the goals, beliefs, and principals that consistently support your commitment to the plan itself. If the boundaries and limits this plan places around your sexual life don't fully address the concerns that brought you to recovery in the first place, then you are bound to fail. Prior to writing out a detailed sexual plan, it can be helpful to make a short list of all of the reasons you want to make changes in your sexual behavior.

Eli's list serves as a good example of this first step in the process:

Goals (overall guides to my future sexual boundary plan)
- I don't want to get arrested again.
- I don't want to be embarrassed at the gym again.
- I don't want to wonder if I have infected someone with HIV.
- I want to try dating again.
- I don't want to lie to any more people I care about.

- I want to stay away from situations where I might be tempted to use party drugs.
- I want to go back to school.

After you've stated your personal goals as in the example above, the task of creating a sexual boundary plan becomes clearer. Let's examine how to structure a plan that deals with both the addictive problem and related areas that need attention.

THE PLAN

The Inner Boundary: This boundary is the absolute definition of sobriety—the bottom line. *The inner boundary defines the most damaging and troublesome behaviors that need to be stopped immediately.* These behaviors (not thoughts or fantasies) are the bedrock issues that define your sobriety; if you engage in any of them, you've had a slip. These absolutely include but are not limited to illegal sexual activities, sexual behaviors that violate the rights of others, intensely compulsive sexual activities that repeatedly threaten your emotional or physical health, and sexual or romantic situations that violate agreements or commitments you've made to partners or loved ones.

The Middle Boundary: This defines actions or situations that you know will lead back to acting out sexually. *This set of boundaries lists people, places, and experiences that can trigger your sexual acting-out.* This part of the boundary plan helps to define all of the situations that can "set you up" to engage in problematic sexual activity. This area does not list sexual activities themselves but is more a roster of "warning or danger signs." Examples of items that belong on this list might be certain gyms where you always "end up" going into the steam room for sex or the use of drugs that can lead you to act out sexually. Former sex buddies might be on this list, along with lovers who have been abusive. This is a list of people and situations to avoid—a reminder of when to be on guard and a guide toward positive change. Also included on this list are nonsexual stressors that can contribute to compulsive behavior. Overwork, no exercise, lack of sleep, poor self-care, excessive worry over finances, and difficult family relationships are all examples of contributing stressors that can lead you to act out sexually.

The Outer Boundary: *This establishes the rewards you can expect from being in sexual recovery.* This final list should offer inspiration and a concrete vision of the improvements and other positive things to come in your life. It should list all the activities, hopes, and dreams you have for yourself (or that you want to start dusting off) when you are not acting out sexually.

One of the first things every recovering sex addict gains more of—especially at the beginning of the recovery process— is time. All the time and energy that went into cruising, flirting, and sexual acting-out can now go toward other purposes. The items on this list can be immediate and specific—such as "painting my apartment" or "taking a comedy class" or "going to more movies." Or they may be long-term and/or less tangible: "beginning to really understand my career goals" or "studying meditation and journaling" or "having a better relationship with my friends."

This list should reflect a healthy combination of work, recovery, and play. If working out every other day, going to support groups three times a week, and seeing a therapist regularly are going on your list, then you need to balance those worthy objectives with spending time with friends, seeing movies, and pursuing creative hobbies. It's important that healthy pleasures take up some of the time you formerly devoted to the intensity of sexual acting-out.

Eli, whom we met earlier in this chapter, talks about how finalizing a sexual boundary plan helped simplify his sexual choices:

> Though I found it quite frustrating at times, once I had the plan set up, it was easy for me to be very clear in the moment—I had no doubt about what was and was not okay for me to do sexually. My plan helped me to eliminate the number-one previous challenge to my staying sexually sober, which was impulsivity. With this written plan in place, I no longer made sexual decisions based on how I felt in the moment, the availability of a given, or how hot a guy was. Instead, I started making sexual decisions based on a plan that has its foundation in my ongoing belief system. And it has become my "gold-standard" reference tool.

SAMPLE BOUNDARY PLANS

Below are two sample plans to guide you in creating your own. All plans vary according to the needs and situation of the individual. Some areas may seem redundant, but it is more helpful to be extremely *thorough and detailed* in defining your plan rather than overly general. **A plan should always be the product of earnest conversation and commitment between you and at least one other recovering individual, therapist, or trusted friend. You should not change your plan unless you've consulted one of these individuals.** Lovers and significant others are not usually the best people to consult since the issues related to these plans are often potentially volatile. A close sexual relationship tends to amplify this volatility. Sometimes it is difficult even for good friends to truly be direct with you.

<u>SAMPLE</u> <u>BOUNDARY</u> <u>PLAN</u> <u>#1</u>

Keeping in mind the goals outlined by Eli above, let's consider a sexual boundary plan that he wrote to address his concerns and interests. Note that Eli included not only negative things he wanted to avoid but also some positive directions he wanted to move toward. Both elements are important in the development of a sexual boundary plan.

Eli's Goals
1. I don't want to get arrested again.
2. I don't want to be embarrassed at the gym again.
3. I don't want to wonder if I have infected someone with HIV.
4. I want to try dating again.
5. I don't want to lie anymore to people I care about.
6. I want to stay away from situations where I might be tempted to use party drugs.
7. I want to go back to school.
8. I want to learn how to spend time alone comfortably.

ELI'S SEXUAL BOUNDARY PLAN

Eli's Primary Boundaries:
Bottom-Line Sobriety (Sexual Behavior Only)
1. I will not go into the wet areas of the gym (sauna, steam, shower, Jacuzzi).
2. I will not go to any sex clubs or bathhouses, adult bookstores, or sex shops.
3. I will not cruise public restrooms.

4. I will not go to bars alone.
5. I will not have unsafe sex or sex (oral or anal) without using a condom.
6. I will not have sex with someone without knowing his first and last name.
7. I will not have sex with someone without knowing him for at least two hours.
8. I will not have sex in any public places.

Eli's Middle Boundaries:
Warning and Trouble Signs/Situations That Can Jeopardize My Sobriety

1. Cruising the gym workout areas without talking to people
2. Going to the park or mall alone
3. Drinking too much, then going out alone
4. Lying to myself or others, keeping secrets
5. Isolating, not returning phone calls
6. Working more than 45 hours a week
7. Having a whole weekend open without plans
8. Fighting with my boss
9. Spending more than a few hours with my parents
10. Holiday Season
11. Not going to therapy or my support group
12. Avoiding exercise
13. Not getting enough sleep
14. Skipping meals

Eli's Outer Boundaries:
The Rewards and Maintenance Steps That Will Help Me Keep My Sexual Sobriety

1. Start evening classes.
2. Attend 12-step meetings three times a week.
3. Start planning weekly volleyball game with friends,

consider joining a gay team.

4. Make meals for family and friends at my place.
5. Stop carrying around the feeling that I'm going to get caught or get into trouble.
6. Play uncle to my nieces more often.
7. Stop needing to worry about getting a sexually transmitted disease.
8. Feel good about being on time and not having to apologize for being late to everyone.
9. Work out every other day (no weekends!).
10. Make a phone list of other recovering guys and use it!
11. Attend to my financial health and stability—start a savings account.
12. Buy movies for my home collection with money I used to use for acting out sexually and porn.
13. Begin daily journaling and possibly meditation.

SAMPLE BOUNDARY PLAN #2

Josh, who is in a primary relationship with his partner, Allen, provided this plan, which meets his goals and also serves his relationship and sobriety.

Josh's Goals

1. To not have sex outside my primary relationship
2. To stop masturbating compulsively—no masturbation with porn
3. To be honest with Allen
4. To improve my sex life at home
5. To work toward having a family and children together

JOSH'S SEXUAL BOUNDARY PLAN

Josh's Primary Boundaries: Bottom Line Sobriety (Sexual Behavior Only)

1. No paying for sex in any form
2. No prostitutes, escorts, or sexual masseurs
3. No going to sexual chat rooms or viewing online porn
4. No sex with anyone other than Allen
5. No e-mail or instant message communication with anyone who interests me sexually or romantically
6. No masturbating by myself—masturbation is to be a shared activity with my partner
7. No looking at any porn videos or magazines or going online for porn in the workplace

Josh's Middle Boundaries: Warning and Trouble Signs/ Situations That Can Jeopardize Sobriety

1. Lying or keeping secrets from anyone
2. Looking at the back of the local arts paper at the massage and escort ads
3. Looking online at hustlers and bodybuilders
4. Going online after Allen and I have a fight
5. Getting up and going online after Allen has gone to bed
6. Getting phone numbers of guys who I think are hot or giving out my cell phone number
7. Staying at work after everyone else has left
8. Intense sexual fantasy, excessive sexual objectification of others
9. "Surfing" the cable TV channels hoping to catch something sexually hot
10. Skipping my support group meetings or therapy
11. Saying to myself that I'll just look at the porn but I won't masturbate to it

12. Feeling overwhelmed, scattered, or guilty
13. Isolating myself
14. Breaking commitments to myself, Allen, or others

Josh's Outer Boundaries: The Rewards and Maintenance Steps That Will Help Me Keep My Sexual Sobriety

1. Going to therapy on a weekly basis—both group and individual
2. Attending my 12-step meetings
3. Getting a sponsor and writing my steps
4. Being romantic with Allen—flowers, baths together, mutual massage, making meals for each other
5. Investigating child adoption
6. Looking at houses to buy on the weekends
7. Bringing our families together with meals, parties, events
8. Taking a pottery class
9. No more HIV tests!
10. No more secrets!
11. Going to movies and ball games
12. Reinvestigating going back to school

Now create your own sexual boundary plan.

My Goals

1.

2.

3.

4.

5.

6.

7.

8.

MY SEXUAL BOUNDARY PLAN

My Primary Boundaries: Bottom Line Sobriety (Sexual Behavior Only)

1.

2.

3.

4.

5.

6.

7.

8.

9.

10.

My Middle Boundaries: Warning and Trouble Signs/ Situations That Can Jeopardize My Sobriety

1.

2.

3.

4.

5.

6.

7.

8.

9.

10.

My Outer Boundaries: The Rewards and Maintenance Steps That Will Help Me Keep My Sexual Sobriety

1.

2.

3.

4.

5.

6.

7.

8.

9.

10.

Reviewed with _____

Date _____

KNOWING YOUR TRIGGERS

A trigger is an individual, situation, or experience that increases your desire to sexually act out and makes it more likely that you will relapse. Triggers leave you feeling impulsive and emotionally aroused. It is *extremely important* to be clear about what triggers your desire to act out.

Before they learn about sex addiction, many men say that they sexually acted out just because they were "horny" or because someone hit on them. They will cite "no particular reason," "the weather," or a certain "mood" as the rationale for deciding to be sexual.

The recovering sex addict learns to identify the particular circumstances that leave him vulnerable to acting out and creates a safety plan to keep himself sober. When he realizes that his addictive behavior has been triggered, he will already know whom to call, where to go, and how to keep himself from violating his sexual sobriety.

While everyone has his own particular triggers (examples of which are listed in the Middle Boundaries sections in the plans above), there are some generic triggers that put nearly every sex addict at risk of a slip. Here are some examples of triggers that increase the likelihood of sexual acting-out:

Generic Triggers
Long periods of unstructured time
Long periods of time alone
Traveling alone
Being left home alone (e.g., for an individual in a
    relationship, when a spouse leaves town)
Holidays and special events
Airports, hotel rooms
Visiting with parents or other relatives
Wet areas of the gym (sauna, showers,
    steam room)
Online bulletin boards, chat rooms, dating sites
Disinhibition from drugs or alcohol
Overtired, overworked
Driving long distances alone
Relationship problems
Financial problems
Pornography
Driving or walking in red-light districts in urban
    areas
Stopping in rest areas, truck stops, mall restrooms
Certain bars, coffeehouses, or other gay hangouts

You should add any of these triggers that are problematic for you to the Middle Boundaries section of your own boundary plan. You should also take time to carefully consider how you can avoid or improve these situations in your life.

CREATING ONLINE BOUNDARIES

Cybersex and online hooking-up is one of the most pressing concerns for all gay sex addicts who are trying to recover. Whether you're captivated by bulletin boards, chat rooms, Webcams, or cyberporn, the lure of that little screen in your den, office, or briefcase can be pretty irresistible. Since using the computer and accessing information online is necessary for nearly everyone, some suggestions for handling the cybersex problem are in order.

While some of the suggestions below apply more directly to some men than to others, following these general ideas will help you avoid the impulsive challenges the computer can create:

1. Delete from your computer files all of your saved pornography, erotic stories, and e-mail. Use the computer's item search function to find material that isn't easily found in other files.
2. Eliminate from your e-mail address book any contact information for men with whom you would act out.
3. Change your screen name and *delete your old one.* Eliminate any screen names or online identities used solely for sexual purposes.
4. Change your network service provider (some providers block access to all porn and erotica sites).
5. Buy and install blocking software to restrict your access to porn, escort sites, erotica, and the like. Get a friend to load the software. He or she should keep the security key number so that you can't impulsively remove the software.

6. Cancel your memberships to porn, escort, and other sex-related online clubs or sites. Get rid of all pay-per-view Web links even if it means canceling the credit card that is used to pay that account.

7. If you live with other people, move the computer to a common area of the house and commit to only going online when others are around.

8. Delete any saved files that could trigger sexual acting-out. These could include written self-descriptions or personal photos that may have evaded deletion while you were doing step one above.

9. Remove your Webcam or any other live video equipment from the computer. *This is essential* if you're to avoid easy access to this kind of interactive activity.

10. Get rid of any pornography or sexually interactive stories that you've purchased on compact disc or stored previously on a disk. Don't look for places to donate it or give it away; just throw the stuff out.

11. Go online for e-mail only. If there is no reason for you to be searching online, don't. Make a written and verbal commitment to avoid any online searching or activity. Let other people gather information or data for you if need be. To ensure your accountability, make calls to other recovering people before and after you go online.

While adding some of these suggestions to a sexual boundary plan will provide many sex addicts with a necessary separation from problem online sexual patterns, others may have to take a more demanding path. Men for whom having the computer at home inevitably leads back to acting out sexually may simply have to take the computer out of the house! Some cybersex addicts—particularly men in early recovery—find that they cannot trust themselves to be alone at home with the computer and its instant access to sexual content. For them, the workplace, coffeehouses, and the public library are safer places to gain brief online access (for e-mail and pertinent information only) as a necessary recovery step.

For addicts who act out online in the workplace, behavior modification may involve turning their computer monitors so that others can easily observe their online activities. Others must ensure that they never stay in the workplace alone after hours.

SEXUAL BOUNDARY PLANS AND RELATIONSHIPS

If you're involved in sexual and romantic relationships, the sexual boundary plan will affect the sex life you share with your partner. Much will depend on whether he is aware of your sexual acting-out and what kind of sex the two of you have been having.

For example, if your relationship with your partner was supposedly monogamous and your partner had no knowledge of how you've been acting out sexually, then it isn't likely that he will experience much difference in your sex life when you begin your boundary plan. If, however, you and your partner have previously been in an open relationship involving threesomes or other types of sex that might now compromise your sexual sobriety, he will clearly be affected by the changes you're making to bring about your recovery. You will need to educate him about your addiction and help him understand why you're changing kinds of sexual behavior that were formerly integrated into your relationship.

Single men will develop a sexual boundary plan based on the kind of sexual and romantic life they want to create for themselves in recovery. The man who has little interest in dating or monogamous relationships will develop a very different kind of plan from the guy who is looking for the ultimate boyfriend and, eventually, marriage. Relationships, dating, and sexual recovery will be discussed more thoroughly in upcoming chapters.

CELIBACY

Some sex addicts are so enmeshed in the compulsions and rituals of their addiction that they're not able to stop acting out sexually without taking a complete time-out from sex altogether. Others—having spent most of their lives in endless patterns of flirtation, seduction, and cruising—need some time to acquire new coping strategies and to get to know themselves better without being sexual.

Not surprisingly, when they stop engaging in these activities, many men find they must deal with uncomfortable and unfamiliar feelings of vulnerability and fears of intimacy—challenges they had managed to avoid for much of their lives. Like the newly sober alcoholic who often doesn't know how to enjoy a party without drinking, the celibate sex addict is forced to deal with his underlying fears of rejection and his lack of interpersonal control and anxiety, all of which were masked by his former sexual acting-out.

Actually, celibacy itself is quite simple. Celibacy simply means no sexual activity *with yourself or anyone else* for a clearly defined period of time. This includes looking at porn, sex with any partners, any type of masturbation—*all sexual activity*. Celibacy is usually most helpful in the early stages of the healing process, and sex addicts may commit to anywhere from 30 days to up to six months of sexual abstinence, sometimes committing to just a few weeks or a month at a time.

Again, this time-out is *not a cure* for sex addiction but a cleansing, self-reflective step toward integrating healthy sexuality into your life in recovery. As with other elements in your sexual recovery plan, celibacy commitments should be written down and your commitment should be reinforced with the help of another individual.

SEXUAL BOUNDARY PLANS—FINAL THOUGHTS

These plans are meant to be somewhat flexible; they are not set in stone. You may spend a month or two with a particular set of boundaries and eventually decide that they need adjusting; this is typical of the recovery process. When you're developing your plan, don't think of it as being forever; just think of it as something for now. Otherwise, the process can be overwhelming. However, changing the rules in your sexual boundary plan is not something you should undertake on your own. When you decide to make changes, you should always engage the help of someone who understands your sexual problems and their context. Never change your sexual boundary plan just because you encounter some hot guy or sexy situation. That is not the time to "freshen up" your plan. More likely, your wish to change your plan under these circumstances is a form of "acting out," and you'll likely have to restart your sexual sobriety time or suffer consequences as a result of your slip.

When you're looking for people to advise you on your recovery, remember that you will always be able to find someone to "sign off" on some sexual activity you still want to do or to agree that it "isn't really a big deal anyway." Remember that the purpose of the plan is not to justify or rationalize your previous behaviors (or some version or them), but rather to bring your sexual acting-out to a close. So when you look for help with your boundary plan, make sure you choose someone who fully understands your history and your concerns and who values the future you want to create for yourself. Find someone who is willing to tell you the truth and who isn't afraid of your disappointment or anger. Remember: In the beginning it's not a bad idea to be a bit conservative about your sexual choices; you can always loosen up your plan later.

Your sexual boundary plan should be specific because that makes it easier to hold yourself accountable to your sexual recovery goals—particularly in the face of challenging circumstances. One characteristic of addiction, particularly for sex addicts, is difficulty in maintaining a clear focus on the big picture when you're faced with the immediate prospect of intensity, stimulation, and acting out. Unless you devotedly follow the clear written boundaries you have established in your recovery plan, you're susceptible to deciding "in the moment" what choices are best. Impulsive decisions won't lead you toward your goals.

These suggestions for how to create a sexual recovery plan may feel comfortable to some people and not so comfortable to others. Some gay men will balk at the idea of placing written limitations on their sexual activities and call the idea sexually repressive or even homophobic. Others will say these steps make life too difficult and get in the way of their fun or other life priorities.

All of this may be true. Some of the steps toward your recovery may seem obvious, trivial, or just plain silly. But keep in mind that your judgment and criticism may be products of your fear of the unknown, a persistent desire to act out, or perhaps fear of failure.

Addicts tend to resist change and resent control. Remember that tolerating emotional discomfort—rather than acting out in response to it—is a major goal of this growth process. Remember too that creating healthy change over time is the objective and that these new practices, even the uncomfortable ones, will serve you better over time than the habits you have been using to deal with your problems.

About Withdrawal

Like many drug addicts who quit using, sex addicts can experience emotional or physical withdrawal symptoms when they stop or change compulsive sexual behaviors. Abruptly ending deeply engrained patterns of physical and emotional behavior is bound to produce some difficulties. This experience can vary in type and intensity among different individuals, but it's good to be aware of some common characteristics that many recovering sex addicts speak about. If you have these experiences yourself, it's important to talk about them with other people in recovery or with friends and family. They are a normal part of the process, but if your discomfort is acute, you should talk to a professional counselor or therapist as soon as possible.

Common Withdrawal Symptoms

The Honeymoon: Some sex addicts entering recovery, especially for the first time, have an initial "honeymoon" experience. This means that suddenly they lose all craving to act out sexually; it feels like they have been cured! Some people who are new to recovery get excited by the insights they're gaining from the books they're reading and the support groups they're attending. Others are stunned and relieved finally to have found a possible solution to their long-term problems (or still shaken from the crisis that forced them to address their sex addiction in the first place). All of them seem to have completely lost the desire to act out their former sexually addictive behaviors. While this break can be an opportunity to gain knowledge, support, and direction, it can also be a source of false confidence. The desire to act out will certainly return—most likely stronger than ever—and if the sex addict doesn't anticipate this, he may later think he did something wrong. It's important to understand that the ebb and flow of addictive impulses are simply a normal part of the withdrawal process.

Switching

Switching from one compulsive behavior such as sexual acting-out to other forms of addictive behavior is common among people who are just beginning their recovery. One common situation is the recovering sex addict who begins to spend or gamble when he gives up his sex addiction. Others may begin to eat compulsively or start intensive exercise programs, while some return to addictions long left behind, like smoking cigarettes or marijuana abuse.

Longing and Craving

For some addicts, sexual acting-out has masked long-suppressed emotions like depression or grief. Without constant sexual stimulation as a distraction, these emotions may manifest themselves in feelings of unbearable loneliness, needfulness, or unhappiness. Many people describe longing for some relationship they feel they will never have or feeling like there is something missing that they cannot find or locate. These feelings are completely normal and to be expected. However, if you find yourself avoiding daily responsibilities like work or family commitments, taking poor care of yourself, or actually having fantasies about not living, it is essential that you get professional help immediately.

Irritability

Some sex addicts in withdrawal typically experience a great deal of irritability and anger over what seem like normal, ordinary challenges. Just as some of the emotions previously masked by sexual acting-out were depressive in nature, other emotions come closer to anger or frustration. It can be a good idea to warn close friends and family in advance that you may experience this kind of emotional reactivity. This will help them to be more tolerant and to take your anger less personally. If you can abide these difficult feelings without getting fired or kicking the cat, there is much to be learned from them. It's common for sex addicts to avoid certain types of confrontation or to repress their angry feelings, only to act them out later sexually. Learning what provokes your anger and how to manage it constitutes a first step toward better self-care and better relationships. Sex addicts in withdrawal are not always fun to be around, but experiencing and learning to tolerate these difficult emotions is an essential part of recovery.

CHAPTER 6
MAKING CHANGES AND FINDING HELP

Growing beyond the underlying emotional patterns that support sex addiction requires more than simply creating a plan to remain sexually sober. Although the work begun in the previous chapter is an essential starting place, maintaining a plan of healthy sexual behavior is not enough on its own to produce long-term change.

The sex addict who is seeking improved intimacy skills and emotional healing must actively work to replace his past addictive behavior with a more robust sense of self and healthier, more supportive relationships. Whether through 12-step recovery, individual or group therapy, or ideally some combination of these options, he must find stable situations that meet his healthy needs for validation, affirmation, and attention. Honest, nonsexualized interactions with other people that allow him to feel accepted and understood are indispensable to the addict's recovery.

These types of situations provide affirmation that he's making healthy changes and that his responses to emotional challenges are improving. If isolation is a hallmark of an active addict, an intimately connected and actively involved support network of caring others *from whom he has no secrets* is a hallmark of his emotional strength and sustained recovery over time.

FINDING HELP

Though many components of sex addiction recovery involve solitude and self-reflection—such as journal writing, reading, or meditation—nothing replaces the insight and accountability that interaction with other people provides. Still, as we touched on in the previous chapter, lovers and significant others are rarely the best people to turn to as a primary source of support in the early stage of recovery.

As important as it is that you're completely honest and transparent with your partners, the challenges of ongoing sexual recovery are too emotionally charged—literally too close to home—for any spouse to be objective about your life and your commitments.

Though addicts often want immediate forgiveness from their partners, it's better to seek help first from another recovery resource. Even longtime good friends aren't always the best people to provide the help and direction addicts most need. So where does a recovering sex addict turn?

The people best able to provide support and guidance are those with similar sexual problems who are also in the process of healing. *These people can most readily be found in 12-step recovery programs for sex addicts or through addiction-focused therapy groups.* Having a handy list of these resources is essential when you feel the impulse to act out, need immediate help, or simply want support and guidance. Including these people in the development of your recovery planning is vital to your success.

HEALTHY RECOVERY CHOICES INCLUDE:

- Involvement in 12-step recovery groups for sex addicts
- Accountability to someone other than yourself or a spouse for your sobriety

- Addiction-based therapy groups
- Individual addiction-focused individual psychotherapy or treatment
- Ongoing relationships with supportive people who know all about your sexual behavior and who are willing to be called anytime when you need help.
- Scheduling your time carefully—particularly on weekends, holidays, or when you're traveling
- A written sexual boundary plan (see previous chapter)
- A disciplined focus on making your recovery a *primary life goal*
- Regular reading of books and other materials about addiction to increase your insight and self-knowledge
- Planned time for spouses or partners as well as friends and family members
- Quiet time for self-reflection, meditation, journalizing, spirituality
- Physical self-care (exercise, nutrition, physician visits)
- A comfortable living environment
- Finding healthy ways to reduce stress

While you may not employ every item on the list above in your recovery, it's important to explore all the strategies that can help to get you back on track when you feel like acting out sexually. At a minimum, your commitment to your recovery must entail engaging other people who have traveled down the road you're on, a written sexual boundary plan, having people to whom you're accountable, learning when you need to reach out for help, understanding more about sex addiction, and slowing down your life to make sex addiction recovery a priority.

12-STEP SUPPORT GROUPS

One of the most useful tools to help you achieve sexual sobriety is a self-help program for recovery from sex addiction based on the 12 steps of AA. The meetings of 12-step groups offer multifaceted opportunities for peer support, shame reduction, and nonjudgmental guidance—along with an ongoing community where you can cultivate hope and change. Small wonder that groups modeled after the 12 Steps of Alcoholics Anonymous (AA) have helped millions recover one day at a time from alcoholism and other addictions such as pathological gambling, compulsive eating, and sexual acting-out.

Still, walking into that first meeting can be one of the most difficult challenges for anyone seeking recovery. Despite the usefulness of 12-step programs, many people are turned off by the prospect of attending or participating in this kind of support group. Whether from ignorance, homophobia, shame, fear of discovery, or the misperception that 12-step groups represent some kind of "religious cult," many addicts would rather "figure it out alone" than attend 12-step meetings.

Unfortunately, trying to "figure it out alone" is exactly what gets most sex addicts into trouble in the first place. While not all the answers to healing sexually addictive behavior are to be found in 12-step meetings, the principles supported by the 12-step programs and the fellowship and support they lend to the recovery process are invaluable to addicts who are committed to recovering. In sum: *All sex addicts who are serious about getting sexually sober should go to 12-step sexual-recovery meetings often* (at least as often as they were acting out sexually), get the phone numbers of people there who are willing to support their sexual healing process, and involve themselves in a community of like-minded people.

Once you resolve to attend a 12-step meeting, you'll realize that anxiety and lack of familiarity with the programs had more to do with your reluctance than anything that actually occurs when you finally get there. There are several different sexual recovery 12-step programs, including Sex Addicts Anonymous (SAA), Sexual Compulsives Anonymous (SCA), Sexaholics Anonymous (SA), Sex and Love Addicts Anonymous (SLAA), Sexual Recovery Anonymous (SRA), and others.

For partners and significant others, there are also support groups that function like Al-Anon—the group for the families and friends of alcoholics. Some of these groups, such as Co-Addicts of Sex Addicts Anonymous (COSA) or S-Anon, can be found through referrals within the recovery communities or online. (See appendix 1 for complete 12-step program information.)

Ed, whose story begins this book, recounts his experiences in 12-step programs:

> At first I felt like there was no way was I going to sit around with a bunch of sleazy strangers and talk about my sex life. I always thought those kinds of groups were sort of cultish anyway. And the last thing I needed was to have my boss or some friend see me walking in or out of one of those places; I'd never hear the end of it.
>
> But after a particularly shameful bout of acting out and more insistent urging from my therapist, I put my fear and ego aside and just gave it a try. I was actually surprised to find that most of the meetings were in fairly neutral locations like church basements or community centers. The meetings were early in the day or after work, so attending them wasn't too difficult.

Most of the guys I met there were actually pretty friendly and didn't demand too much of me, other than that I just sit and listen to their stories and see if we had anything in common. Despite my initial skepticism, I liked the vibe almost from the beginning. It really touched me to hear other men talking so casually about some of the sexual things I had been hiding for so long. I heard guys telling stories like mine, only without all of my shame and self-hatred. Many of them seemed to have genuinely found a way to stop being sexually addictive and had the tools they needed to keep it that way. I could see them having real friendships and nonsexual intimacy.

The more meetings I went to, the more hopeful I started to become. I began to see a way out for me, got some phone numbers of guys I thought could give me direction, and even started reaching out for help. Some guys even started calling me. What started out as a "have-to" became a "want-to" situation—I began to look forward to the honesty, encouragement, and lack of judgment I found at the meetings. Looking back, getting started at 12-step meetings was probably the single greatest contributor to my long-term sexual sobriety.

To try to help allay the fears of people who might be unfamiliar or uncomfortable with the 12-step process, some 12-step group members offer answers below to some frequently asked questions regarding sexual recovery programs.

Q: I've heard that sex addiction meetings can be homophobic and that I will not be supported around being gay or having a same-sex partner. Is this true?

A: Just as in the general population, some people may try to make a particular meeting or group a forum for their own homophobic agenda. However, most meetings have a variety of gay and straight attendees and are quite gay-friendly. Most people attend meetings because they want to stop acting out sexually—not to push a political or other kind of agenda. The best thing to do is go to different meetings until you find a few that feel really comfortable and welcoming. Remember that no one gets to decide what you need to change except you and the people you directly invite into your life to help you. Some meetings are actually specifically for gay men and will be designated that way on meeting listings.

Q: I am concerned about being seen at these meetings and people talking about me because I've been to them. How private is a 12-step meeting?

A: It's ironic that the very same men who risked public humiliation by having sex in parks or mall restrooms think it might be too embarrassing to be seen at a 12-step sexual recovery meeting. While it's true that these meetings are not bound to the same level of confidentiality as a therapy group might be, all participants in 12-step programs are committed to anonymity as part of their own recovery process. Many sexual recovery meetings are restricted to sex addicts only, which can add an extra layer of comfort and safety for the people who attend them. In almost every case, the benefits of attending a meeting far outweigh the possible negative consequences. Remember that whoever might see you there doesn't want to be talked about outside the meeting any more than you do.

Q: I don't want to have to talk about myself publicly. Will they make me do this if I go to these meetings?

A: Other than asking you to introduce yourself by your first name, no one will expect you to participate in the meetings unless you want to. No one will make you share anything that you don't wish to.

Q: I have heard that a lot of freaks and sex offenders go to these meetings. My problems haven't really hurt anybody but myself, and I don't think I would feel comfortable around a bunch of sex offenders.

A: A wide range of people attend sexual recovery meetings—from those who must participate in a 12-step program as part of a sentence for a sex-offense conviction to those seeking help for problems that are harmful to no one but themselves. Believe it or not, there is something to gain from hearing just about everyone's story at the meetings. At the end of each meeting you can decide whom you would like to get to know better and who you want to avoid, whose example you want to follow and whose doesn't make sense for you.

Q: I have heard that there is a lot of emphasis on religion in these meetings. I don't feel comfortable with all that God stuff and I certainly don't want to trade my sexual problems for being involved in a cult. What's the deal with this?

A: The 12-step groups employ phrases like "higher power" and "a power greater than ourselves" to help sex addicts put their faith in something larger than themselves. The word "God" is used as well. Most sex addicts have amassed so many problems and are so desperate for solutions that by the time they get to a 12-step meeting they need to begin to rely on something beyond rather than their own ideas and willpower. Some new members will start out by simply seeing the group itself as an example of a power greater than themselves. But nothing is asked of the newcomer other than the willingness to simply attend and to incorporate into their own recovery whatever works for them personally. The 12 steps themselves do use the word God; however, this reference is not directed toward any specific religious or belief system.

Q: I hear that more people get picked up for sex in those meetings than actually get well. Is it true that the sex addicts meetings are big places to hook up with guys looking for sex?

A: If you're a sex addict looking for sex, you can pretty much find it anywhere. If you go to 12-step meetings looking for the support of people with long periods of sexual sobriety—who can lend a hand to help you—that's what you'll find. If you go to a 12-step meeting in major cruising mode, you'll likely be able to persuade someone to be sexual. In general, the meetings are safe, supportive places. It's always best to keep yourself out in public with new members—either staying in the meeting places or moving your conversation to a relatively open public space, like a coffee shop. It's also best to avoid getting too involved with one member too quickly, since falling into sudden, intense relationships is often a hallmark of sex addiction and romantic addiction. In this vein, it's best not to share too much too quickly with one individual. Sex addicts crave instant intimacy, and there really is no such animal.

Q: What is a sponsor and how do I choose one?

A: Sponsors are personal guides to healing and sobriety. They're usually not friends to begin with and they are never lovers. A sponsor is usually another man who has been involved with sexual recovery long enough to have achieved some success at sexual sobriety himself. He should visibly be involved with the recovery meetings, have written and worked on the 12 steps himself.

You choose your sponsor by listening to various people at the meetings until you hear someone or several people who sound like they fit this profile. In addition, their experiences should fairly closely match yours; this will help them guide you more individually. For example, if you're in a long-term relationship, a sponsor who is in a similar relationship might be preferable to someone who's not. If you're HIV-positive, it might be helpful to have an HIV-positive sponsor. And so on.

You should approach your prospective sponsor, ask him if he is available to sponsor someone, and if he is, propose that the two of you meet to talk about your recovery. This is the best way to start. If he says no, don't take it personally or give up—just ask someone else.

Jeff, 11 months into his recovery, had this to say about sponsorship:

> Getting a sponsor was a bit scary at first, as I didn't quite know what kind of person would be right for me and I was afraid to approach someone for help. I was also afraid of "getting stuck" with the wrong person. Ultimately, I did find the right guy and have found having a sponsor an invaluable part of my recovery program.
>
> When I first started going to 12-step meetings I struggled to find the courage to just get a few phone numbers. Then, actually calling people up and asking for help seemed like an impossible task. Finally, finding one person—my sponsor Patrick—who really got to know all about me and my problem made a huge difference. It gave me someone who was a little further along in the recovery process

than me to ask for direction and guidance.

With my sponsor, I started to feel like someone was there for me 24/7. So when that urge to go and act out came in the middle of the night or during some lonely weekend, I could always call Patrick up and he was there to help out. More than once, making that simple phone call has kept me sexually sober.

GETTING INTO THERAPY

Seeking therapy in conjunction with 12-step support and sexual sobriety is one of the most useful steps to take in recovery. The therapy setting provides a safe place to work through all the feelings and initial challenges that stopping addictive behavior brings up.

Finding the right therapist can be half the battle. In the past, medical diagnoses were used to pathologize homosexuality, and even among professional therapists there's still a fair amount of prejudice and misunderstanding about what constitutes healthy gay sexuality. This makes choosing the right therapist to treat sex addiction more difficult for gay men.

It's essential to choose someone who has a balanced and supportive view of gay men and healthy gay sex along with an understanding of sex addiction. Many gay men who are seeking answers to personal or relationship problems have faced well-meaning but clueless counselors or clergy who either wasted their time or money or worse.

Jared, a gay man who wanted to enlist a therapist to help him with problems *not related to sex addiction*, describes his first therapy experience:

> I first went to therapy because I was having some problems finishing up a project for work and I just

couldn't get past it. I thought a counselor might help me figure out why I was procrastinating so much and what was keeping me feeling so down. I had been depressed around my schoolwork back in college, so I thought that maybe I was getting depressed again.

The counselor in my health care group was really nice, and we had some good conversations about my family life, work, and my relationship with my boss. I felt her concern and caring for me.

But when we started talking about my sex life, it started getting uncomfortable. She knew I was gay from the start and that seemed fine, but as I started talking about circuit parties and some of my after-party cruising her whole attitude changed. I don't think that she meant it, but I could really tell that she didn't approve of my getting into sex with multiple partners. Although I didn't really say that I was looking for one, she started pushing me toward settling down with just one guy. The truth was that I had just broken off a three-year relationship and just wanted to be free again for a while.

When I disclosed to her that I had probably been sexual with 70 or 80 guys, give or take, over my lifetime, she began to turn the therapy sessions toward looking at my sex life. The truth is, my sex life has never been a problem for me, has never gotten in the way of my work or relationships, and I really enjoy it. I began to resent her disapproval and felt really intruded upon. So what if I want to have occasional anonymous sex?

We never really resolved the work-procrastination issue I went to address in the first place.

I left therapy pretty soon after I started and never went back.

Jared's story points toward the underlying homophobic prejudices that can alienate gay clients from some prospective therapists. These attitudes can make it difficult for a healthy gay man to openly explore his sexuality and relationship experiences. They pose even greater difficulties for the man who's already involved in problematic or self-destructive sexual patterns and already ashamed of his sexual behavior.

At the other end of the spectrum are gay men who have sought help for addictive sexual behavior only to find themselves enabled in their behavior by well-meaning, gay-supportive therapists who offer advice such as "Maybe you're being too hard on yourself," or "You should just loosen up and allow yourself to become more comfortable with your sexuality." These responses are entirely inappropriate when the sexual activities a client describes are creating negative consequences in his life. The therapist who offers this kind of advice likely intends to help his or her gay clients overcome homophobia; in any case, these good intentions lead them to exactly the wrong approach for men who struggle with compulsive sexual acting-out.

Carl relates this story:

> Even after I lost a job I really liked because I was using the computer at work for sex, it was hard to get my counselor to take the issue seriously. All of the hours I should have been preparing for the next day or just plain sleeping I was either online masturbating to porn, hanging out in the chat rooms, or hooking up for sex.
>
> Because most workdays I was either too tired

or too irritable to concentrate, I would slack off and try to get away with doing less or just leave early. Looking back, now I can see that I needed someone to help me stop those sexual behaviors and challenge me on my thinking. At the time it was really easy to buy into what my friends were telling me; I wanted to believe that what I did was the same as everyone else, even though deep down I knew that it wasn't. It's hard to blame other people, though, because I'm not sure I was willing to listen at the time either.

The therapist I saw at the local gay and lesbian center didn't seem to see a problem with my sexual behavior. Despite my complaints about the time, energy, and even physical injury my masturbation habits were causing me, he just kept insisting that I shouldn't be so hard on myself, that I was struggling with homophobia, and that when I was more self-accepting, I would feel better about my sexual behavior. Finally, after several months of this—and after I kept getting worse—I asked to see someone else.

Despite ongoing evolution in the field of addiction research, sex addiction remains a poorly understood disorder—even by many mental health professionals. Although 25 years have elapsed since the publication of Patrick Carnes's groundbreaking book, *Out of the Shadows: Understanding Sexual Addiction,* many professionals—including sex therapists—have scant experience treating addictive sexual behavior. In particular, sex therapists are mostly trained to help people who have problems enjoying or engaging in sex rather than those who are addicted to it.

Choosing the right helping professional can be confusing.

The choices are many: psychiatrist (MD), psychologist (Ph.D.), licensed sex therapist, master's level counselor, licensed social worker, addiction counselor, and pastoral counselor. When you're choosing someone to help you begin to recover from sex addiction, a more important consideration than a counselor's academic degree is whether he or she has training in and knowledge of sex addiction, or at least a general understanding of the treatment of addictive disorders.

A good way to start looking for a therapist is to listen and talk to other people at 12-step sexual recovery meetings. By spending time with sex addicts in recovery who seem to be doing well, you can get a sense of what is working for them. Many of the people you'll meet may already have counselors or know of treatment centers where they've formed successful, supportive therapeutic relationships. Most recovering people are happy to tell others about their therapy experiences and offer helpful recommendations.

Another excellent resource is the Society for the Advancement of Sexual Health (www.sash.net). It maintains a list—organized by country and state—of professionals who are knowledgeable about sex addiction. Therapists who have expertise in sex addiction are the ones who'll most likely be able to help you; even then, you should ask them to describe their experience and comfort in working with gay men.

Many of the nationally known drug and alcohol treatment centers maintain lists of therapists who are trained in sex addiction treatment. Addiction treatment facilities can provide the names of knowledgeable therapists in your community, as can the gay and lesbian community centers found in most urban areas of the United States. Many larger corporations and most unions offer workers access to employee assistance programs (EAP). EAP counselors often have addiction training, though they may not be knowledgeable about sex addiction.

Sex addicts who have health insurance should check their insurance plans to see what diagnoses are covered and what therapists they can use. Unfortunately, many plans do not cover treatment for sexual issues. People who suffer from sex addiction often also struggle with anxiety, depression, and work or relationship problems; you may be able to request a referral to a therapist for those issues.

EVALUATING A THERAPIST

The most important part of your evaluation of a prospective therapist is paying attention to how meeting with them makes you feel. Do you feel understood? Do you feel like this individual has the knowledge to help you? Do you feel like the therapist was being genuine and real when he talked about his experience with other people with your issues, or was he trying to impress you? Did he take the time to really listen to you or was he more interested in hearing himself talk? *Did you get the sense that he is willing to confront you about behaviors and activities you know are unhealthy, or do you worry that he might allow you to make serious mistakes without challenging you on them?*

QUESTIONS TO ASK A PROSPECTIVE THERAPIST

To determine whether a therapist is able to handle sex addiction issues (and whether he or she seems at ease with your sexual orientation), evaluate the therapist's experience by asking questions. *Don't be afraid to ask a prospective therapist questions* about training, background, and past work. You should feel comfortable discussing the length of time your treatment may take, the frequency of your meetings, and the fees the therapist expects. This meeting does not, however, commit you to therapy with that individual. You may wish to "interview" several people before you make up your mind as to which professional might best meet your needs. Addiction treatment differs significantly from traditional therapy, and you should be sure a prospective therapist hears your particular concerns and possesses the relevant experience to help you in your recovery.

Questions to consider asking prospective therapists:

- Do you understand sex addiction?
- Have you ever treated a sex addict?
- What is your experience with sex addiction, compulsive sexual behaviors in general, and other addictions?
- Do you recommend that your clients attend 12-step meetings?
- Are you familiar with the concepts taught in Alcoholics Anonymous and related programs?
- How would you support my sexual sobriety?
- How would you help me if I acted out sexually?
- Are you comfortable working with gay men's issues?

THERAPEUTIC CHOICES

While many therapists prefer to work in one-on-one individual therapy with their clients, once a client has been fully evaluated, *the preferred method of treatment for most addictions is group therapy*. If a therapy group for sex addicts is not available, many aspects of the 12-step support group can be used to supplement individual therapy.

Seeing a therapist as an outpatient while you're attending supportive 12-step sexual-recovery meetings is a strategy that works quite effectively for most people. Addicts who experience a severe emotional or life crisis related to their addiction or those who are unable to stop acting out sexually despite professional outpatient help and 12-step support may require a residential, inpatient or outpatient intensive treatment program. These intensive treatment settings offer a higher level of care than you can get from simply going to an outpatient therapist's office or attending 12-step meetings. They are designed for addicts who are struggling with profound depression or anxiety in addition to their addiction.

But in most cases, the best first step is to meet one-on-one with a well-trained professional. He or she can then help guide you in the process of recovery.

COUPLES THERAPY

Couples who've been traumatized by the recent revelation that one partner is a sex addict need a special kind of support—especially if the addicted partner's acting-out has involved extensive deceit or betrayal. Therapists who advise that the partner who has been betrayed "should just leave him" or "kick him out" miss the point that many partners—even those who've suffered a tremendous shock at the level of their significant other's acting-out—may not want to give up their relationships over it.

When you're seeking a couples therapist, it's important to find someone who can hear your story without imposing a hidden agenda on the course of your therapy. The addict—who's so eager for forgiveness in the beginning of therapy—needs the therapist's help to contain his anxiety and fears of abandonment so that the partner he betrayed doesn't end up being the one to soothe and reassure him.

The right professional can help a couple negotiate the early stages of recovery by directing the addict toward the recovery strategies that he needs while supporting the spouse through the hurt and anger he may be feeling. A good couples therapist guides a process of disclosure and helps to reduce the power of long-held sexual secrets.

Jeff, the partner of a sex addict, talks about his experience with couples work:

Couples therapy allowed me to access truths about our relationship that Richard had covered up for so long. As much as I hated hearing it, I needed to know everything that he had lied about—a disclosure process was essential. It helped me stop blaming myself and allowed me to see the kind of problems Richard had been dealing with, even before we met. Later, when I wasn't so angry, I began to examine how closed off I had become to him and to myself; how I had slowly accepted living with someone who wasn't emotionally there and what that had cost me. I think it really helped us for Richard to be present to hear my end of the story and for both of us to learn what to do differently if we were going to go forward together.

Sometimes a couples therapist will work with each member of a couple in individual therapy and also see the couple together. More rarely, and usually less successfully, the therapist will see only one member of the couple for individual therapy.

At some point early on, the therapeutic relationship and the therapist's office must become a safe place for the addict to disclose his sexual history so that his partner isn't left in the dark about what has been going on in the relationship. The therapist can help the other partner communicate any feelings of hurt, loss, and anger. When you're dealing with concerns this sensitive, it's best to seek out a therapist who's thoroughly versed in treating sex addiction and who has provided help to couples in the past.

Situations where both partners have sexually acted out can also make good use of couple's therapy. The partners in this type of couple can learn to redirect their sexual recovery, creating safe new ground rules regarding sexuality and intimacy.

FINDING HELP OUTSIDE URBAN AREAS

Life in the big city offers many opportunities for individuals to act out sexually, but it also provides the recovering sex addict many places to go for help. People living outside urban areas, however, have fewer support resources to choose from. Still, this doesn't mean that help is unavailable to people living in smaller cities or rural areas. Here are some useful suggestions to those living in less densely populated environments:

- Several 12-step sexual recovery programs have *online meetings* and offer long-distance peers and sponsors who can be contacted by phone and/or e-mail. Many recovering people participate in regular weekly online chats, gaining strength and support from others around the world. People without Internet access can connect by phone. Many programs regularly publish newsletters and other reading materials that are usually available through the mail or online.

- Most 12-step programs hold annual conventions in different parts of the United States and around the world. These provide a great opportunity to connect with others.

- Some therapists are willing to consult with clients over the telephone or by e-mail, and many of these professionals are easy to find online.

- A great deal of reading material devoted to sex addiction is available through online bookstores, libraries, and even small local bookstores. See appendix 2 for a list of recommended books.

THE KEY TO MAINTAINING CHANGE

As any successfully recovering addict will tell you, the keys to changing addictive behavior are quite simple:

- Acceptance of your problem
- Initial motivation to change
- Willingness to ask others to help you
- Staying motivated
- Accountability

Those who are committed to avoiding a return to their sexual acting-out will tolerate rituals and situations that are sometimes annoying and unfamiliar, experiment with uncomfortable and difficult feelings, and make themselves accountable to people they barely know. They're willing to take this arduous path because they don't want to continue to suffer from an active addiction that shapes their lives.

People who've suffered a trauma as a consequence of their addiction—an arrest or a crisis involving their health or a relationships, for example—and who've cultivated a real commitment to reclaiming their lives from addiction are the ones most likely to stick with the recovery process and experience long-term change in their behavior. Addicts who appear to enter recovery but simply want to appease an upset boyfriend or boss, accommodate a court order, or "feel better about themselves" while they continue to act out sexually soon discover that living a hidden life while acquiring new self-awareness is a very uncomfortable situation. At some point they will either have to fully commit to changing their sexual behaviors or end up returning to the very patterns of addiction they sought to change in the first place.

MAKING SENSE OF SLIPS AND RELAPSE

Robert reports that thinking he had his problem solved put him right back where he started:

> Just prior to my slip, I had been actively working for nearly a year to manage my anonymous sex and prostitution habit. Before recovery, it was not unusual for me to spend three to four hours a day driving around the boulevard looking for younger guys to pick up or cruising the adult bookstores. During my first few months in recovery, I was involved in therapy, attended multiple 12-step meetings weekly, and diligently worked at learning to manage my problem. I slowly began to regard my past sexual behavior as a symptom of a difficult time in my life that was now ending.
>
> When I passed the nine-month mark in sobriety, I gradually became less serious about earlier commitments, such as avoiding driving down certain streets on my way home from work or avoiding staying late [at work] by myself. I started going to fewer meetings and took a time-out from therapy. Somehow I had never found the time to end my membership at the adult video store in my neighborhood like my therapist recommended or get rid of that one e-mail address where I used to get porn, though I always said I'd get to it.
>
> One Saturday morning, when I was feeling overwhelmed from the workweek, I thought, "I should really just relax today and take some time for me. I deserve it." So I slept in instead of going to my regular weekend morning 12-step meeting. Then it occurred to me I should take out my bike

and go for a ride in the park. I told myself that I really needed some exercise now that the weather was getting warmer. The fact that I was headed toward some old cruising grounds never consciously crossed my mind.

I stopped and bought some food to enjoy in the park and complimented myself on what a good job of self-care I was doing—not considering the challenge inherent in the place where I was putting myself.

I had barely locked up the bike and begun to eat my sandwich when I saw some guy lying around in the sun with his shirt off, and that was it. After spending the next two and a half hours cruising the johns, having anonymous sex, and nearly getting arrested, I felt pretty miserable.

It didn't take me long to realize—once again—that I didn't have any real control over my behavior. Unless I consistently and thoroughly follow the plans that have been suggested to me, I'm not going to get well and stay well.

Robert's story demonstrates that sex addicts often end up having slips by convincing themselves that they have fixed the problem or that they're cured. Robert didn't deliberately head out to the park looking for sex—though by reviewing the situation and writing about it, he recalls feeling mildly excited when he begins to toy with the thought that he's *entitled* to skip his 12-step meeting. "I deserve to be able to have this time to myself to go out to the park. I have been working so hard. It's a good reward." Robert's story highlights some important signs of impending relapse.

KEY WARNING SIGNS OF RELAPSE

- **Overconfidence:** "This has gone really well for a few months—maybe I have the problem solved."
- **Isolation:** Spending several days without contact with other recovering people, skipping support groups or meetings
- **Blaming others:** "If my boyfriend hadn't gotten a job that took up so much of his time, I wouldn't be so lonely and tempted by other guys."
- **Justifying or rationalizing slippery situations:** "I could wait to take a shower when I get home, but the showers are so much better at the gym and I had such a good workout. Besides, I'm in a hurry."
- **Minimizing a return to problematic situations:** "It's not like I'm hooking up with guys on the street anymore. I'm just getting a sensual massage. Besides, massage is good for me."
- **Avoiding or devaluing feedback:** "That therapy group just wants to control me—they're just a bunch of sexually repressed losers." "What does my sponsor know? It's not like he's single and has to be alone like me."
- **Comparing yourself to others with different degrees of sexual freedom:** "Every other gay guy gets to go to the bars and get as much action as he wants. If I get a lot of looks and hot guys are into me, I don't see why I should deprive myself. What's the point in that?"
- **Ignoring previously agreed-upon guidelines:** "That boundary plan doesn't make sense for me when I travel. It really only should be in place when I'm at home."
- **Entitlement:** "Look how hard I have been working at the office! What difference does it make if I look at a few videos here and there? I deserve some fun too."

- **Using recovery to justify acting out sexually:** "I'm not perfect. I'm entitled to have a slip once in a while. I don't have to be a recovery poster child!"

SLIPS VS. RELAPSE

Many sex addicts will recognize themselves and their thinking in the examples above. It's a normal part of the recovery process for the addiction to "fight back" once in a while as you work toward healing. And while you must not use slips as an excuse to relax your vigilance, they may occur for some.

A *slip* is a brief, mostly unintended return to acting out sexually. Sometimes an unexpected stressor or a poorly managed or maintained recovery plan will lead to a sexual slip.

It's important to distinguish a slip from a relapse. A slip can be managed and contained by immediate, honest disclosure of the event, followed by a revised plan to shore up your resolve to stop acting out. If you're in a relationship, a slip is something you must tell your spouse about so that you don't create any new secrets—no matter what the cost.

Relapse occurs when a sex addict is unwilling to be honest about his slip and begins to hide and justify his behavior, thus setting the stage for slips of increasing frequency. Hidden or ongoing slips, lies, isolation, and a return to a secret hidden sexual life can all define relapse.

The moment you catch yourself having a slip or in the midst of a relapse, *check in with your sponsor, reach out to one of the people on your 12-step list, or call your therapist.* You've established relationships with these people to enlist their support in your day-to-day recovery and to throw you a lifeline if you fall back into your addiction. Ask for help! It's yourself you're saving.

CHAPTER 7
FOR PARTNERS AND SPOUSES

While sex addicts face some serious challenges in their effort to get sober, their boyfriends and life partners likely have it even harder. Although some partners are comfortable with open relationships, it is a rare individual who can remain indifferent once he learns the true extent of his significant other's sexual acting-out. Even the most laissez-faire partner would have trouble dealing with the kinds of consequences that addictive behavior inevitably creates.

Today, as many gay men in long-term relationships are beginning to see the value of openness and commitment for their emotional well-being, most boyfriends and partners are devastated when they discover they have been betrayed by men they love. Partners' feelings often veer from anger to compassion, and it can be confusing to figure out what feelings to express at what point in an ongoing, very difficult conversation.

As a partner, most likely you're usually supportive when your significant other has a problem. But what do you do when your spouse's problem causes you to confront a history of lies and betrayal from someone in whom you have placed the most trust?

If betrayal occurs, many partners mentally review and call into question everything they thought they knew about their relationships, looking back to try to figure out what they missed and what went wrong. For someone who believed he was in a monogamous relationship, the revelation that he has been betrayed on a vast scale may prompt him to wonder what, if anything, was true about his relationship with his partner. He may begin to doubt that he and his partner can reestablish the kind of trust they need to continue to make a life together.

Jeremy (whom we met in chapter 4) talks about what it was like for him to come home one day to find his lover, Juan, having sex with a prostitute. Later he learned that Juan had acted out sexually throughout the course of their supposedly monogamous five-year relationship:

> I went through waves of feelings in the beginning—all the way from hating him and wanting him to leave to understanding that he had a problem and wanting to be supportive. Finding out about his sexual secrets did help me understand some of his past moodiness, constant lateness, and swings from being distant to sometimes incredibly loving.
>
> But I was left with a big question as to what we had really had together at all. Was everything a lie? Looking back, how could I even believe the times when he had said, "I love you" or "I want to be with you always"? How could those things have been true if he could walk out the door an hour later to have sex with some stranger at work or the gym?
>
> I am not one of those guys who can do non-monogamy, and Juan knew that from the very beginning. Yet he agreed to monogamy! Was that just to please me, or did he really mean it?

Even though he was frequently looking over my shoulder to check out other guys and sometimes even flirting with them while we were together, I had always just written it off as just a gay thing or even a guy thing. Now that I know he's a sex addict, I'm revisiting my own feelings and acknowledging that I often felt less than important when we were in a crowd or around other attractive men. His frequent comments to me about how hot this, that, or the other boy was—while his head was swiveling from one man to the next—always left me feeling less than. I just never felt before like I had the right to confront him about it. Now I'm wondering why I didn't ask more questions and speak up sooner.

Jeremy is beginning to question *himself* as he looks back on his history with Juan. It's not unusual for partners of sex addicts to go through this kind of self-investigation as they try to integrate the real facts of their relationship into the healing process. This is a way to grieve the loss of what they thought their relationship had been. Just as someone who has experienced the sudden death of a close friend or parent may wonder whether more could have been done to enrich the relationship with that individual, partners often feel remorse when they consider how they might have acted in the past. It's all too common to think, *Somehow, if I had just done it differently, maybe my partner wouldn't have been with those other guys.* Or, *Maybe if I were younger or more attractive, he wouldn't have done this.*

Some partners begin to examine feelings and misgivings they may have pushed aside in order to justify the behavior of the addicts in their lives. Their own feelings of shame and embarrassment along with the sexual nature of the problem often prevent partners from reaching out to get the support they need. This isolation only adds to their difficulties. Jeremy continues:

> At first I didn't know whom to talk to about this or where to turn. I felt like maybe it was my fault—maybe I hadn't been a good enough lover—and I was embarrassed that other people might think that as well. Besides, whom do you go to when your lover—your best friend!—has betrayed and violated you? It wasn't something I was going to call up my sister about, or the guys at work—especially since I had spent the better part of four years telling everyone how well things were going in my relationship and that, yes, gay men could be happy together over the long-term.
>
> Part of my hesitation to talk about what had happened had to do with my fear that everyone would just tell me to get rid of Juan, and I didn't want to. Despite my anger and hurt I didn't want to hear anyone else's opinion that I should leave him or kick him out.
>
> Instead, I got hungry for information. I went out and read every book I could on the subject of betrayal and sex addiction. I wanted to understand the problem so that somehow I could fix it on my own, make it right for both of us. I also did a lot of detective work. I started going through his things—his wallet, credit card receipts, and cell phone charges—looking for clues. It was as if I thought that if I knew everything or could anticipate anything, then somehow I would be able to

predict the outcome, to know how it would all turn out in the end for us.

At some point, however, I got tired of the whole thing being focused on him—his acting-out, his emotional problems, his shame and embarrassment. What about *my* loss, *my* pain, *my* fears about the future? I got tired of asking him about *his meetings*, how *his* sobriety was going, and if *we* were going to be okay.

I found myself becoming more critical and unpredictable, expressing my anger sideways through sarcasm, nagging and emotionally withholding from him. It seemed like I was just angry all the time, no matter how hard he was working on his recovery. I started to dislike myself. That's when I finally decided to get some help for me.

UNDERSTANDING YOUR FEELINGS

In trying to help the spouses and partners of sex addicts, many friends, family, and even therapists fail to understand that, despite the betrayal and violation that has occurred, a lot of love remains at the core of these relationships. Many people listening to the partner's side will counsel him to get out of the relationship right away. They don't realize that integrating all the difficult information that has been exposed by the betrayal takes time; usually, it's wisest for the betrayed spouse to put off any major life decisions that would simply make him feel more off balance.

As we saw in Jeremy's story, the very individual who betrayed him was the same person he leaned on for support, guidance, and direction. So leaving right away, for most partners, is usually not a good option.

Still, most betrayed partners go through a wide range of feelings about the addict. All of these feelings are reasonable and appropriate—and none of them need to be acted on right away.

NORMAL PARTNER RESPONSES TO FINDING OUT ABOUT THE PROBLEM

Shock or Numbing: While other people around the spouse may be filled with outrage or anger, the spouse is simply numb or confused. His first impulse may be to seek comfort from the usual source: most often, the sex addict himself. Cut off from his usual touchstone, the partner just can't fully comprehend what has happened.

Remorse and Self-doubt: "What did I do to cause this and why didn't I see it coming?" As we saw in Jeremy's story, many spouses turn their anger and hurt inward on themselves. They blame themselves for not seeing the patterns of deceit, for not having more insight into their partner's emotional experience, and think that if they had been a better (thinner, smarter, richer) partner, the problem wouldn't have occurred. In order to impose some measure of control over the pain and loss of this situation, they place blame on themselves.

Honeymooning: Some partners will try to avoid the pain of the present by moving into the romance mode. "Now that I know the truth we can finally be close. By making love and being sexual now, we can forget the problems of the past. If we have a lot of sex, he won't need anyone else."

Hatred Toward Third Parties: If the sex addict had affairs, the partner directs the blame toward the individual (or individuals) involved in the affair (or affairs). The addict somehow becomes the "innocent victim" of someone else's unscrupulous behavior.

Unpredictable Emotions: Understandably, the betrayed partner will experience periods of anger and mistrust toward his spouse; sometimes, seemingly for no reason, he'll become angry or withdrawn. Just seeing a sexy image on a billboard or watching a steamy scene in a TV program might trigger feelings of rage and fear when moments before the couple had been getting along.

SEX AS A QUICK FIX (THE HONEYMOON)

Some couples who want to restore "intimacy" in their relationships will turn to sexual intensity or romantic "honeymoon" experiences to try to quickly recreate some closeness in their relationship following the disclosure of a sex addict's problem. It's not unusual for couples that have had relatively distant, dispassionate sexual relationships to get into hot or intense sex with each other following the disclosure of betrayal and sexual acting-out. While sexual and romantic intensity may feel good for the moment and provide each partner some measure of reassurance, sex used as a means to soothe difficult feelings enables both partners to avoid deeper, more troubling issues. The "honeymoon" experience is a form of mutual denial that is bound to fail.

It's healthier, though less comfortable, to engage in a "cooling off period." This involves a mutual agreement not to cycle into any sexual or romantic intensity and to put off any longer-term decisions—like whether to break up or permanently change residences—until there is more clarity about where things are headed. It's essential to take some time—90 days is a commonly suggested period—to grieve the past, to learn more about addiction and addictive patterns of behavior, and to work on honest modes of communication and healing through support groups and couples and individual therapies before making any major relationship decisions. After this period of hard work and healing, it's more likely that decisions about the relationship will be carefully considered and therefore minimally disruptive.

PARTNER ISSUES IN NONMONOGAMOUS RELATIONSHIPS

For some men, one of the advantages of being gay is having more options for relationship partnering than the traditional "heterosexual model" of a monogamous marriage. Because gay relationships aren't so bound to constructs geared toward propagating the human race, a gay man may choose a variety of ways to explore sex with other people while still cultivating a primary relationship with one other individual. For this reason, sex addiction can be harder to identify in a nonmonogamous relationship. Therefore, it's necessary to examine the characteristics of *a healthy nonmonogamous relationship.*

Most counselors who work in the field of intimacy and healthy sexuality agree that a nonmonogamous relationship can only work when there is a clear, well-defined agreement between the partners that establishes how the sexual arrangement is supposed to work for that couple. Here are a few examples of how the rules for a nonmonogamous couple can look:

1. Either partner can have sex with whomever he wants outside the relationship, but *both partners agree not to discuss these sexual encounters.*

2. Either partner can have sex with whomever he wants outside the relationship, but *both partners commit to discussing their experiences.*

3. Each partner can have sex with other people, but the partners must *discuss and agree on these sexual encounters in advance.*

4. The partners will only have sex outside the relationship when *other people are brought in* (i.e., threesomes).

5. The couple (either individually or together) will *only have sex with people they know.*

6. The couple (either individually or together) will *only have sex with anonymous strangers.*

7. Each partner can have *single sexual encounters with another individual*—no reliable fuck buddies or ongoing romantic situations outside the relationship.

8. Partners living in separate homes are *monogamous when they are together and nonmonogamous when they are apart.*

Gay (and many straight) couples can and do experiment with different forms of nonmonogamy, with varying results. Problems develop when each of the lovers has a different notion of what the sexual arrangement is—or the couple simply hasn't agreed upon a plan at all. Misunderstandings of this type tend to breed resentment, hurt, jealousy, and other bad feelings that can severely damage an otherwise functional relationship. Couples who have agreed to a mutually understood plan of sexual behavior yet who still find themselves contending with broken sexual promises or sexual secrets may need to consider (a) whether nonmonogamy really works for them and (b) whether the sex addiction of one or both partners is the cause of the trouble.

Two of the identifying characteristics of sex addiction are living a double life that involves deceit and sexual secrets and consistently breaking promises about your sexual behavior that you make to yourself or other people. It's possible for two sex addicts in a relationship to enable one another's problematic sexual behavior when neither partner has the objectivity to identify his own problem or that of his lover. This kind of situation can go on for years until a severe consequence from sexual acting-out compels one or both partners to change.

Bjorn talks about his relationship in this regard:

> We practically lived in the parks, Chris and I. After work, the park was the first stop we would make together. Each of us was off cruising to find someone to pair off with in the bathroom or bushes. Sometimes we would bring guys home to share. I would say we spent at least three or four hours a day cruising and getting into or having sex with other guys.
>
> On weekends, if we didn't head back to the park, we would often go out to cruisy beaches or to the bathhouse together. The search for sex was absolutely our main hobby. Even when we would get home after cruising and sex, one or both of us would often be online in the chat rooms or sex sites trying to find someone to score with later in the evening or the next day.
>
> Of course there were consequences. On more than one occasion over the years I ended up getting "bashed" by some homophobe asshole looking for someone to hassle, and there were several arrests for "public indecency." Despite this, back we would go to the same place where I had been beat up or arrested just a few days before, grumbling about the damn cops or the jerk-off kids with bats who were probably closet cases themselves.

It wasn't until I lost my job that I started to look at the sex as a problem. Since I had some money put aside, I decided to put off looking for work for a while, but "a while" became weeks, then months. Because I wasn't working, there was no reason not to go out to the park, so I just decided to go at it full-time. Before long I was cruising most of the day, every day, for what eventually amounted to well over 45 hours a week.

This didn't really affect me too much because there was still money in the bank, but I did notice all the time it was taking. Then one night when some guys looking to scam drug money in the park beat up Chris so badly that I didn't think he was going to make it, I finally started to think that maybe our sex life was becoming a problem.

Even so, it was many months before I went to see a counselor and even longer before I was ready to consider a change in my life. The hardest part for us was that Chris didn't want to stop or change his sexual behavior, even though I knew I just had to. This issue nearly broke us up until we finally got into couples counseling and began to address our sexual choices as a part of our relationship and not something we could just deal with separately.

Couples like Chris and Bjorn face considerable challenges when both partners are used to being very active sexually and one of them decides that he wants to make a change. This one-sided commitment to change is bound to put the whole relationship under tremendous strain and force the couple to reevaluate their priorities and commitments. As Bjorn's story suggests, such a couple usually needs the guidance of a professional to help them work through deeply engrained belief systems and patterns of sexual behavior.

ABOUT CODEPENDENCY AND COADDICTION

The partners of most sex addicts strongly resent any suggestion that they might also have a problem. And why wouldn't they? For men who are dealing with the hurt and anger of betrayal, the overwhelming impulse is usually to assign blame to the partner who caused the hurt. It's easy to understand why the betrayed spouse might believe that the man who broke the promises and withheld painful secrets is the source of the problem—not the man who has been victimized or violated by the situation.

While it's true that the sex addict has a great deal of work to do to address his compulsive need for validation and self-soothing through sex and to take responsibility for the consequences of acting out sexually, partners also usually have issues that need to be addressed. Not surprisingly, their problems are often more subtle than the overt activities of the sex addict.

Men who partner with people with addictive personalities often have underlying emotional deficits that are similar to the issues of the addicts to whom they're attracted—their unhealthy responses to emotional challenges simply play out differently. In contrast to the addict's need for constant validation and attention, the partners of addicts can seem rather selfless to outside observers, while beneath the surface they struggle with underlying fears of being abandoned or deemed unlovable. While these concerns may be largely unconscious, they profoundly affect the sufferer's relationship choices as well as his behavior in the context of a relationship.

The spouses of addicts often appear most comfortable when others depend on them and they will sometimes go to great lengths to try to become indispensable to the people in their lives. Unaware of their deep lack of self-esteem, these men seek out people and situations that enable them to be givers. This role is comfortable and familiar because it has usually been learned in chaotic or emotionally neglectful families where the ability to make others happy was an important survival tool.

While being a giving human being is generally a positive attribute, co-addicts often give too much—*often doing for others what others could be doing for themselves*. While a co-addict may be underrested, overtaxed, and overcommitted, his primary aim is to please and take care of the people around him and to avoid conflict and dissatisfaction. Unaware of his own emotional (and sometimes physical) needs, he will invest inordinate amounts of time and energy to "be there" for others. All the while he stores up deep reserves of anger and resentment as his own needs go unmet.

This hidden or shadow side of the co-addict partner shows up in the indirect ways he expresses his resentment and feelings of victimization. He vents his negative feelings through blame, nagging, sarcasm, criticism, passivity, and emotional or sexual withdrawal, leaving his partner and other people around him feeling guilty, hurt, or angry and also without a clear sense of how to restore harmony.

Co-addicts are usually angry with themselves as well as their partners. They don't like how negative they've become in their attitudes and in their relationships to other people, but they have no idea how they arrived in such a negative space. Some co-addicts become dependent on overeating, drug use, compulsive exercise, spending the addict's money, or other potentially self-destructive behaviors. They develop these dependencies as a way to fulfill their own unmet needs and to soothe their deep sense of frustration. By trying to address their problems this way, co-addict partners set themselves up for what can become lifelong struggles with body image, weight, or finances.

HOW DO I KNOW IF I'M A CO-ADDICT?

Some past and current partners of sex addicts developed the following list of questions to help them understand their common problems. You can use these questions to determine how your relationship to someone with a sex addiction may have affected your life. Answering affirmatively to three or more of the questions is an indication that you should seek a professional counselor with whom you can discuss these concerns.[1]

1. Have you often felt hurt, ashamed, or embarrassed by someone else's sexual conduct?
2. Are you afraid to upset your partner for fear that he will leave you?
3. Have you sometimes found yourself searching for clues about someone else's sexual behavior?
4. Have you ever fantasized, obsessed, or worried about someone else's sexual problems?
5. Have you ever made threats to others or promises to yourself like "If this happens again, I'll leave" that you did not carry out?
6. Have you ever tried to control somebody else's sexual thoughts or behavior by doing things like throwing away pornography or being flirtatious or sexual with him in order to keep him from being sexual with others?
7. Has your involvement with another individual or his sexual behavior ever affected your relationship with your friends, coworkers, or family members?

8. Have you often lied to others or made excuses to yourself about another individual's sexual conduct?

9. Have you had money problems because of someone else's sexual behavior?

10. Have you engaged in sexual behavior that makes you feel uncomfortable or ashamed or that is physically dangerous because you fear that if you don't your partner will leave you?

11. Have you ever felt confused and unable to separate what is true from what is not true when you're talking to your partner?

12. Have you ever thought about, threatened, or attempted to commit suicide because of someone else's sexual behavior?

13. Have you often used sex to keep the peace or to smooth over problems?

14. Does sex (thinking about it, having it, talking about it, or worrying about it) play an all-consuming role in your relationship?

15. Have you ever felt abandoned emotionally because of your partner's use of pornography or masturbation?

16. Have you ever helped someone get out of jail or deal with other legal trouble as a result of his sexual behavior, or feared that this kind of thing could happen to someone else?

17. Have you often blamed your partner's sexual behavior on other people, such as friends or other sexual partners? On gay culture? On his job, religion, or family?

18. Do you feel alone in your problem?[1]

Although the consequences of sex addiction are unwelcome and painful, the means that both members of a couple choose to deal with these problems can be a source of healing and hope. The partners of sex addicts have many choices for how to handle what has happened in their relationship. They have the same prospects for self-healing and many of the same recovery opportunities available to them (therapy and 12-step support, for example) as their addicted spouses.

ABUSIVE RELATIONSHIPS

It's not unusual for couples who are contending with an addiction problem to have to face other dysfunctional behavior as well. Next to drug and sex addiction, domestic violence is one of the most prevalent and destructive problems among gay men. Many men have difficulty verbally expressing anger, hurt, and frustration, and some of them resort to physical violence or intimidation as a means of expressing these difficult feelings.

Hitting your lover or being hit by him in anger is never acceptable. The law is quite clear in this respect: People who lash out physically, whether they are gay or straight, can be arrested if someone reports their behavior to the police.

Besides physical violence, there are many ways to shame and frighten a lover that are just as unacceptable. Throwing and breaking things, pinning someone to a bed or wall, refusing to let someone leave by blocking a doorway, or stalking someone by foot or car are all forms of intimidation that indicate the perpetrator has a serious problem that needs immediate attention. Verbally threatening to kill or hurt yourself or your spouse when you're upset is a form of emotional blackmail that also warrants immediate help.

Relationship violence should never be ignored. If the problems underlying this form of acting out aren't dealt with through therapy, the aggressive behavior will always return in one form or another. If this kind of violence is going on in your relationship, you should speak with a professional right away. Most urban mental health centers, gay and lesbian community centers, and private therapists have resources to help you deal with this extremely serious but treatable problem.

PARTNER RECOVERY

Partners who have experienced betrayal have good reason to feel angry, mistrustful, hurt, and confused. If you are the partner of a sex addict and choose to stay in that relationship, it will be some time before either of you can reestablish real trust and comfort. If the sex addict in the relationship is committed to recovery, then this kind of healing is possible. Your joining the addict in his efforts by starting your own process of self-examination will facilitate healing for both of you.

In the meantime, you have to deal with the emotional fallout and unhappy consequences of your spouse's sexual acting-out. As you try to cope with your hurt and anger, you should take whatever action you need in order to take care of yourself. This self-care may reasonably include asking the addict to move out for a period of time, stopping sexual relations for a period of time, sleeping in separate rooms, or even taking a time-out from the relationship.

It makes perfect sense for you to want to protect yourself in response to your partner's lies and betrayal. In addition, there's no guarantee that the addict in your life is being completely truthful with you, even if he has entered treatment or sought 12-step support and begun to acknowledge his problem. Therefore it's essential that you take steps to tend to your own emotional and physical needs. In the following pages you'll find some dos and don'ts that will help you develop strategies for your own self-care.

THE DOS

1. **Do get tested for STDs (and not just HIV).**

   Most sex addicts are careless about their sexual health and the sexual health of their partners when they are acting out. Later, seeking to hide their behaviors, they lie (sometimes even to themselves) about the health risks they have taken in their sexual pursuits. And HIV is not the only concern. Sex addicts are frequently exposed to a variety of diseases including hepatitis, venereal warts (HPV), syphilis, gonorrhea, chlamydia, and herpes, to name but a few. Once your partner has disclosed that he has been acting out sexually, you should go to your physician and tell him or her about the situation so that you can take steps to ensure your complete physical health.

2. **Do learn everything you can about addiction, codependency, and sex addiction.**

   Read books and articles on addiction and recovery, attend workshops, and look online. There are many resources that will help you learn about sex addiction and partner issues (some of them are listed in the appendix). Make use of as many of these resources as you can. Get educated about sex addiction and the recovery process not only to understand your partner and teach him about sex addiction but also so that you can make informed decisions about your own life.

3. **Do reach out to others for help.**

   If you suspect or are certain that your partner is a sex addict, get help *for yourself*. Regardless of whether you feel you have issues of your own to address, simply living with an addict requires a level of emotional support that is beyond the life experience of most people. Find a support group for partners or co-addicts. There are many 12-step groups like S-ANON, COSA, and CODA (see appendix 1 for a full listing) that are specifically designed for the spouses of sex addicts. There you will find other people who know firsthand the pain, shame, and confusion you're experiencing. The 12-step programs for spouses will help you to understand more fully what your addict is experiencing so that you don't feel so left out of his recovery process. These programs offer an organized way for you to educate yourself and get support. It's also very helpful to make use of counseling professionals who are trained in sex addiction and to consider couples therapy, if your partner is willing.

4. **Do examine your own sexual history and behavior.**
   Sex addicts sometimes come in pairs. If you also have a history of sexually addictive behavior—either within or prior to your current relationship—you may need to address addiction issues as well. Read literature about sex addiction with an open mind and be willing to acknowledge your own addiction if your behavior fits the standard profile.

5. **Do express your feelings and hurt.**
   If you've just discovered that your partner is a sex addict, you're likely overwhelmed with disappointment and hurt. It's not your job to protect your partner from those feelings. In fact, hearing how his sexual behavior has affected the people he cares about is vital for his healing and recovery.

6. **Do trust your feelings and observations.**
   If you don't feel safe with your partner, trust yourself.

If you don't see your partner getting *ongoing* help with his sexual behavior problems—attending therapy, going to 12-step support groups—then don't trust that things are getting better. His promises to change or stop his behavior mean little, but his actions toward change mean a lot.

7. **Do expect your lover to tell you everything about his sexual acting-out.**

You have a right to know what has gone on during the course of your relationship. You should expect that at some point early in his recovery your partner will share the complete history of his sexual acting-out (if you wish to know it) so that you can fully integrate what has happened into your new understanding of your relationship. *There should no longer be any secrets between you.* If your partner isn't forthcoming with this history, you should request it yourself.

THE DON'TS

1. **Don't nag, complain, devalue your partner, or be self-righteous.**

You should express your hurt and upset feelings, but don't subject your partner to an endless barrage of criticism or emotionally withholding silence. Either he is going to embrace honesty and the need to change his sexual behavior or he isn't. Reinforcing his shame and guilt will not help him—nor will it help you!

2. **Don't become a detective or parole officer.**

It doesn't really serve your interests to snoop through your partner's bank statements, phone messages, or computer files. Try to plan in advance how you want to handle the discovery if you should *accidentally* come across information that suggests your partner has not changed his behavior.

3. **Don't use sex or romance to try to "fix the problem"** (as discussed above).

4. **Don't worry that getting angry with your partner or pushing him away with your anger is going to "make him act out."**

   If he wants to act out sexually, he will. No amount of hurt or frustration from you is going to make him do anything. *You are not responsible for his behavior—ever.*

5. **Don't go on a sex binge to "get even."**

   Whatever problems your spouse has and whatever problems you have together, causing more hurt or engaging in more betrayal or secrecy will only make things worse. "Getting even" only feels good for the few moments you're doing it and it usually brings disaster in the end.

6. **Don't handle the situation by yourself.**

   Reach out to sympathetic friends, family members, and support groups. It's not your job to hide your partner's bad behavior or to keep his secrets. Doing either of these things will only isolate you and exacerbate the problem. It's okay to talk to people who know both you and your partner—even at the risk of embarrassing your partner. You have the right to get help wherever and however you need it. His problems are not a reflection on you.

7. **Don't tell people about the situation just to humiliate your spouse.**

   It's one thing to enlist people to give you the support you need; it's quite another thing to tell your partner's mother, boss, or best friend about his sexual behavior just to get even. Eventually, you'll regret that course of action. You and your partner can discuss what information you both consider private and with whom you want to share the information you're both willing to disclose. Develop a personal "press release" that you both agree to stick to.

8. **Don't stick your head in the sand.**

   If you have an investment in your relationship, you can't avoid the hard facts of your partner's sex addiction. Even if you choose to leave the relationship, you need to consider what attracted you to an addict in the first place so that you don't have a similar experience with another individual in the future. Pretending the problem will go away will definitely not make it go away. And placing all of the responsibility for dealing with the problem on the sex addict is simply a way for you to avoid dealing with your own problems.

9. **Don't make threats you don't intend to carry out.**

   Make certain that you do whatever you say you are going to do. If you say that if he acts out sexually again you're going to leave, then if he acts out, you'd better have your bags packed. In other words don't rashly say things that you wouldn't say after careful reflection. Otherwise, you diminish your credibility. In any case, it's usually best to not make threats at all.

PARTNER RECOVERY PLANNING

Learning that your partner is a sex addict is bound to put you in crisis mode. Many partners have to manage unpredictable mood swings, difficult feelings, and the consequences of the sex addict's acting-out (which can include diseases, affairs, or major financial problems).

To create some stability for yourself, you should develop a

clear plan of action for self-care and for dealing with day-to-day interactions with your partner. You can use this plan as a guide to help you make decisions when your anger might prompt you to make choices you may later regret or when depression or confusion makes it difficult to take actions that would steer you toward a more levelheaded place.

Max, who found out about his partner's sexual acting-out four years into their relationship, describes how he developed a plan and how his plan facilitated his healing process:

> When I first found out that Will had been having several affairs, I just wanted to get rid of him and move out. I didn't want to tell anyone. I just wanted him and the whole thing—especially my hurt—to go away. Now I'm so grateful that I turned to a recovering friend of mine, Amy, who took me to my first S-Anon meeting.
>
> Though I kicked and screamed about having to attend "one of those programs" and said "why should I take my time to do this when *he was the one with the problem*," looking back, I have to say it was probably the best thing I could have done for myself. There I found comfort in the stories of other men and women who had been betrayed by their partners and who had found a way to continue their relationships and heal. I also found a way to talk about my fears and anger without having to completely shut down and isolate with ice cream and television.
>
> At the 12-step meeting I got phone numbers from a few other men and women who were in similar situations as me, and they guided me through the worst initial few weeks. One of these

men later became my sponsor and he suggested that I write out some rules to follow for the next 60 days. It really helped to have a simple plan:

My First 60 Days
- Attend 12-step meetings twice a week.
- See a therapist.
- Don't end the relationship because of a bad feeling.
- Don't make up or believe information unless I have facts.
- Write down my questions for Will in my journal and go over them with someone else before I confront him.
- Phone a friend at least one time in the evening before bed.
- Go back to the gym three times a week to keep my stress down.

The best part of the process for me was that it gave me some guidance for when I felt out of control, and it kept me from isolating in a way that would have harmed me further.

As the spouse of a sex addict, you need to remember to be gentle, patient, and forgiving *with yourself*. Remember that there is no easy or right way for a couple to handle something as emotionally difficult as a sex addiction problem. No one does this perfectly. Many couples do work through their troubles, however, and most couples can stay together and overcome self-destructive habits if both partners are committed to change, seek outside support, and honor a loving appreciation of each other that goes beyond the immediate crisis.

Remember, too, that some partners decide that the violation they've experienced is greater than their desire to remain in the relationship. For them, trust cannot be restored. You're not necessarily bad if you choose to leave an addicted partner, just as you're not necessarily wrong if you choose to stay in that relationship. Most important are the lessons you acquire from learning to trust your instincts and to take better care of yourself.

CHAPTER 8
UNDERSTANDING LOVE ADDICTION

"Scratch most sex addicts and you'll find a love addict underneath."

—12-step program adage

While many sex addicts lose themselves in patterns of sexual compulsivity, some repeatedly enter intensely challenging "love" relationships. People whose addictions lead them toward this kind of behavior are ultimately seeking the same intensity and finding many of the same unhappy consequences as the active sex addict. *Some recovering sex addicts, having halted their patterns of sexual acting-out, turn from the desperate search for sex to a desperate search for a relationship.* Unless they've addressed their underlying emotional problems, this pursuit of relationship will produce as much unhappiness as their pursuit of sex.

Though the main focus of this book is sex addiction, love addiction—which entails emotional and physical arousal stimulated by romantic intensity and obsessive involvement with unavailable partners—closely mirrors sexually addictive behavior and is a related form of acting out. To people who haven't suffered the pain of this particular form of mental illness, "love addiction" may sound more like a topic for daytime talk television than a serious emotional issue requiring intervention. For the love addict, romantic intensity and sexuality, as well as the emotional drama they offer, are more likely to produce fear, anxiety, and pain than genuine intimacy.

Neal, who spent 12 years in a relationship, talks about how his love addiction pattern became apparent:

> I never saw myself as "having a problem." I never was out in the bars, sex clubs, or having anonymous sex. In fact, I was years into a stable relationship with one guy, and I was fairly happy. But periodically I would meet up with someone outside my relationship and just lose myself to him. For whatever reason I would be attracted to a particular man, start an affair, and then it would become balls-to-the-wall intense. Meeting at all hours, hiding and keeping secrets, feeling that if we weren't speaking every day or if I didn't hear from him or see him my world was going to end.
>
> These affairs were like roller-coaster rides. I would lose sight of my priorities and I didn't care who got hurt or how it affected my relationship, work, or friendships. I just wanted to see this guy, have sex with him, and lose myself, even though somehow I usually knew that the feelings for him somehow weren't real. Talking on the phone and planning a get together would make my heart race and my blood pound; each guy was like a drug. After my third affair with a man like this, my partner had finally had enough. It took his packing up my bags and kicking me out to finally wake me up to the problem I have.

LOOKING FOR LOVE

While he's often competent in daily work and social life, the love addict suffers from an underlying, unacknowledged longing to feel special in a relationship. This deep longing reveals a chaotic and sometimes desperate emotional world filled with fears of abandonment, rejection, and unworthiness. The love addict's choice of men who aren't emotionally available, or who are ultimately unattainable for other reasons, reflects his essential belief that love and stability are never to be found. This unexamined belief compels him into an endless search for the "right guy," even if he is already in a relationship. Ultimately, his greatest fear is that he will end up alone, having been found flawed and undeserving of love.

Charles, 32 years old and "still single," reflects on his romance addiction:

> What finally got me to look at this as a problem was my obsession with Internet dating. Once I put up an ad or two I started checking every night and then twice a day to see if anyone had responded. Every time I replied to a new ad my hopes would go up and I would wait to see if this time I might just find "him." Sometimes I would stay up until three or four in the morning repeatedly poring through the old and new ads for anyone that I might have missed and hoping to find someone to send my photo and story to. I wasn't really looking for sex, though I was ready to go for it if I thought it would lead to some kind of relationship. Before I totally lost myself to the Internet, I had tried dating clubs, video dating, the bars, speed dating— you name it. Sometimes I tried having sex right away, and when that didn't work I became

adamant about not having sex right away. I joined organizations and churches that didn't interest me for the sole purpose of meeting available men, and I berated my friends for not introducing me to more potential partners.

The point is that I did none of this for me, to support me, to educate or define me. Nor was I particularly hopeful that I'd meet someone to enhance my life. All of this emotional energy went into trying to find "him," someone else to make me feel complete. Once I found "him," I thought that everything would be okay, that I would be okay.

Forever searching for "the right" guy, the love and relationship addict's intrigues, flirtations, demands, sexual liaisons, and affairs leave a wake of emotional destruction and negative consequences behind him. Ironically, he may have already had many opportunities for the loving experience he truly wants, but the love addict is much more strongly attracted to the intense experience of "looking for love," "falling in love," "the guy who needs fixing," and "the drama of the problem relationship" than to peaceful intimacy.

He is usually left with few options to resolve these painful circumstances except to engage in still more searching, which creates an escalating cycle of desperation and loss. Just when he begins to feel "safe" in the rush of a new romantic affair or liaison, the troubled love addict grows steadily more unhappy, judgmental, and uncomfortable with what he has found. He usually ends up pushing his newfound partner away with criticism and overbearing efforts to control the relationship. Or, if he remains in the relationship, he may find himself longing for a better or more fulfilling "love" or sexual experience.

Thus the cycle begins anew.

LOVE ADDICTS AND RELATIONSHIPS

Sex addicts engage in high-intensity cruising, fantasy, and sexual experiences—often anonymously and very frequently. By contrast, love addicts are attracted to the same level of intensity (and are usually just as detached from the reality of their situation) as sex addicts, but they're usually focused on one individual or relationship at a time. For them, *this man* becomes the sole object of their focus and needs, often to the exclusion of outside interests and support. Instant emotional bonds, formed through intensity rather than intimacy, make an unstable foundation for what often becomes a very unhealthy situation. Like the sex addict—who gives up time, health, and self-esteem in his pursuit of a sexual high—love addicts seeking or involved in new relationships neglect their personal interests, hobbies, exercise, self-care, and sometimes even their jobs to devote more time and energy to an idealized partnership.

Paul talks about his most recent spiral into this pattern:

> I knew Carl was the guy for me from the first time I saw him out on the street. We cruised each other, started talking, and the hours just flew by. I remember having this feeling of completely losing myself in being with him right from the very beginning. I was sure it was love.
>
> Within weeks he became the most important thing in my life. Friends and work took a backseat to any time we could get together to talk, make love, and be together. The sex we had glued us together—it was overwhelmingly intense, and I felt whole and loved. When we were apart, I spent endless hours analyzing every facet of our conversations and experiences together. What time I did spend on the phone with friends was

usually devoted to driving them crazy talking about Carl.

I totally stopped paying attention to the things that made me feel good about me. *My* work, *my* hobbies, *my* friendships all became subject to Carl's availability and his need for my attention. I let that happen. As I let go of what supported me and gave Carl and his happiness more of my focus, how he treated me and whether or not he loved me increasingly became the primary source of my self-esteem.

If we were doing well, I was on top of the world, but in the back of my mind I was worried about what might go wrong. When he would push me away, I would do whatever it took to try to make the relationship work again, even if it felt like I was going against my own values and beliefs. If he was doing drugs, I would do drugs. If he wanted to have sex with other people, I would go along with that too.

What blows my mind is that I never really took a good look at who Carl really was. I was so focused on whether he liked me, whether I was important to him, what I could do to make him happy, that I wasn't looking to see if I even really liked or respected him. I ended up feeling more like a child wanting to please a parent than a partner in an adult relationship. When it finally ended, I was devastated and had little support remaining to fall back on. Because I had so readily given myself away as we went along, when the time came to reclaim me, there wasn't much left to find and I didn't feel like living. That was how I knew I had to seek help. I knew couldn't survive another breakup like this one.

The experience of feeling more like a child than an adult in a relationship is a sign of love addiction. Paul, above, acted out the role of a child whose sole focus is getting a parent figure (Carl) to love him and never leave him. Not surprisingly, Paul grew up in a family with a verbally abusive and devaluing father who was constantly yelling at him, his brother, and his mother. His unexamined trauma of having to please an angry, unavailable dad to keep the peace while doing whatever was needed to get the love that might be available was a deeply ingrained childhood experience that Paul carried into all of his obsessive adult love relationships. He finally began to unpack some of this emotional baggage when he got into therapy and SLAA (Sex and Love Addicts Anonymous).

Not surprisingly, Paul's obsessive behavior also took a toll on Carl. Over time, the objects of the love addict's focus begin to resent the control, dependency, and people-pleasing that are aspects of the addictive personality, and they find ways to emotionally distance themselves. This only reinforces the love addict's belief that eventually he will be left or abandoned.

Below is a list of some telling signs of love addiction. While all romantic relationships may exhibit some of these characteristics occasionally, love addiction is distinguished by a consistent pattern that combines these kinds of problems with severe consequences from cyclical unhealthy behavior.

Typical Signs of Love Addiction:

- Mistaking intense sexual experiences and new romantic excitement for love
- Constantly craving and searching for a romantic relationship

- When in a relationship, being desperate to please and fearful of the other's unhappiness
- When not in a relationship, feeling desperate and alone
- Inability to maintain an intimate relationship once the newness and excitement have worn off
- Inability or difficulty in being alone
- When not in a relationship, compulsively using sex and fantasy to fill the loneliness
- Choosing partners who are emotionally unavailable and/or verbally or physically abusive
- Choosing partners who demand a great deal of attention and caretaking but who do not meet emotional or physical needs
- Participating in activities that go against your personal values in order to please or keep a partner
- Giving up important interests, beliefs, or friendships to maximize time in the relationship or to please a romantic partner
- Using sex, seduction, and manipulation (guilt/shame) to "hook" or hold onto a partner
- Using sex or romantic intensity to tolerate difficult relationship experiences or emotions
- Missing out on important family, career, or social experiences to search for a romantic or sexual relationship
- Using anonymous sex, porn, or compulsive masturbation to avoid "needing anyone," thereby avoiding all relationships
- An inability to leave unhealthy or abusive relationships despite repeated promises to oneself or others
- Repeatedly returning to previously unmanageable or painful relationships despite promises to oneself or others

Pia Mellody in her groundbreaking book, *Facing Love Addiction,*[1] describes three distinct behavioral symptoms of a love addict in a relationship:

1) Love addicts assign a disproportionate amount of time, attention, and "value above themselves" to the individual to whom they are addicted, and this focus often has an obsessive quality about it.
2) Love addicts have unrealistic expectations for unconditional positive regard from the other individual in the relationship.
3) Love addicts neglect to care for or value themselves while they're in the relationship.

THE LOVE ADDICT CYCLE

When searching for love is more about avoiding desperate loneliness than about finding a valued other, partner choice becomes distorted. Cementing yourself to another man so that you can feel whole rather than expanding your world to include someone unique is a setup for an addictive relationship. Compatibility in such a relationship then comes to depend on "whether he will leave me," or "how intense our sex life is," or "how I can manipulate him into staying," rather than on whether the other man is an emotionally independent companion and lover.

Addictive relationships are characterized over time by unhealthy dependency, enmeshment, guilt, shame, and various forms of acting out. The denial of a love addict can be seen in how *he avoids responsibility for his troubled relationships* while looking for the source of the trouble everywhere but in his own behavior. The rationalizations a love addict uses are manifold: "All gay men are liars and can't be honest." "He was just using me for the sex." "Dating younger men is the problem—I'm never going to date guys in their 20s again." "I can't trust men to be honest with me unless I am checking up on them 24/7." "Men are just going to use me if I get close to them."

Placing the blame for his misfortune on the date, the lover, the partner, or the spouse keeps the love addict from having to look at his own desperation. This willful blindness to his own experience traps him in the same cycle of behavior that caused his unhappiness the last time.

Unlike the man seeking partnership and sex as an enhancement to his life, *love addicts seek partners whom they can get to depend on them in some way.* It's almost as if by caretaking for troubled, needy, addicted, or otherwise challenged men, he tries to offer the object of his obsession the attention he never received himself but always wanted. When these problematic partnerships inevitably fail to meet the love addict's own emotional or physical needs, he may become demanding, critical, and even more controlling with his spouse. In any case, the addict will try to get his partner to love him the way he wants to be loved, regardless of whether the other individual is capable of this kind of love.

If the love or relationship addict can't get what he wants, he may begin to act out sexually—starting again to search for "the one" who can meet all of his needs. Or he may avoid sex and relationships altogether for a time—in essence becoming "sexually anorexic." Some men become both love addicts and sex addicts.

Love addicts often find themselves becoming people they don't like—constantly nagging, complaining, or blaming their emotionally unavailable partners for their own unhappiness as they themselves become drained, frustrated, and angry. When they act out their disappointment through sexual compulsion or other kinds of compulsive behavior, they eventually end up with the same feelings of shame, self-hatred, and worthlessness from which they wanted to escape in the first place. Like people who are addicted to drugs, sex, or gambling, love addicts use the fantasy, physical intensity, and endless drama in their difficult relationships to distract themselves from their own emotional hurts. Desperately terrified of abandonment but equally fearful of true intimacy, many love addicts will stay in unworkable and unmanageable relationships long after they have ceased to be a source of any genuine affection or warmth.

BECOMING AWARE

Many recovering love addicts reflect that much of their adult lives had been focused on the search for sexual and romantic partners *in every situation*. Looking back, they can see that they were always prepared and ready to meet someone—they always had some strategy or another in play to find and keep a new partner.

Alex described his behavior and state of mind:

> I don't think I could ever really relax when I was going to a social event if there was any possibility of hooking up. I would spend hours before going deciding what to wear or how I should look. The focus was not on how I wanted to look or what made me feel good, but on what might get a guy interested in me for sex or a date. When I would talk to guys or flirt, I remember being very careful to watch for anything they said that would tell me what they liked or what they were about. Then I would "work" the conversation so that they would really feel like I understood them or was like them. It seems so weird now looking back, because I wasn't really having a mutual conversation; it was more like being manipulative.

Whether by being clever and flirtatious or outright seductive, love addicts are always on the hunt for special attention and intensity—to have the light of a new male connection shining on him. An important part of the healing process is his recognition of the methods he has used to attract and manipulate the attention of others, whether through his wardrobe choices or the way he involved himself in conversation and social interactions.

As he begins to consciously cast aside these ploys using the support of 12-step members, friends, and therapy, he begins to learn his true value as an individual, which diminishes his need for superficial, objectified, or sexualized attention. Alex continues his story:

> Before I got into recovery and started looking at my love and sex addiction, I never realized how focused I was on constantly trying to attract men—how much I had turned myself into an object. Practically everything I wore, the way I carried myself, what I had to say—not to mention all that time spent at the gym—all of these things had little to do with my own self-esteem. Instead I viewed them through the filter of whether I thought they would get some guy to desire or notice me.
>
> A big part of my recovery has been refocusing my attention on what makes me feel comfortable about how I look, what I wear, and whom I choose to spend time with. I have deliberately—but not without a great deal of struggle—taken the emphasis off what might get me male attention, sex, and a boyfriend and moved toward what's fun, relaxing, and puts me at ease. Interestingly, now

that I'm a year into my recovery, I think I might actually be more ready to have someone in my life than I ever was before. But even if "he" never comes along, I'm beginning to get a better sense of what fun is for me—what I like and enjoy. I could never see that before because I was so focused on looking for "him."

Just as recovering sex addicts need a clearly defined plan of healthy sexuality, so the love addict—regardless of whether he's in a relationship—needs a written, carefully organized plan of action that reflects his healthy beliefs about relationships and sexuality. Successfully altering deeply ingrained patterns of addictive love relationships without reliable sources of support will be very difficult. Behavioral change requires becoming accountable to people who know and understand you within a consistent supportive environment. 12-step support groups, group therapy, and individual therapy are places where some of that guidance, support, and accountability can be found. Organizations like Sex and Love Addicts Anonymous (see Appendix 1 for information) provide an opportunity for love addicts to break the cycle of addictive relationships and receive direction from members who have also "been there."

FINDING RELATIONSHIPS THAT WORK

For people who are seeking a long-term relationship, romantic intensity is the catalyst that sparks the playful exploration of possibilities with a special new human being. The beginning stages of a potential love relationship can be the most exhilarating. This is the time when what he looks like, how he walks, talks, eats, and breathes are the subject of endless fantasy and excitement. Most people can easily relate to that "rush" of first love and romance—the stuff of countless songs, greeting cards, and movies.

More than intense romance or sex, however, companionship, honest communication, and acceptance are the hallmarks of healthy intimacy and are the essential building blocks of long-term commitment. *Intimacy is the experience of being known and appreciated over time—one individual's discovering the true inner life of another—more than feelings of immediate intensity or excitement.* True loving relationships develop when partners use the early, exhilarating times as a gateway toward deeper, long-term closeness. It's that deeper closeness and recognition that actually satisfies the seemingly endless longing for something more than you already have. As intensity fades, a new, even richer experience begins.

Alex recalls:

> I used to date guys for a few months, and as soon as the sex got less intense or I started losing the buzz about them, I just figured that he wasn't the right guy—that it was time to move on to someone else. I thought that if the sex slowed down that meant that he wasn't truly for me and I would start looking elsewhere. No one ever actually told me that the passion that sparked the beginning of my relationships doesn't last for most people, straight or gay. Only recently have I come to realize that romantic relationships can deepen, becoming more meaningful and fulfilling over time.

KNOWING YOUR RELATIONSHIP NEEDS

Some written exercises can be quite useful to help love addicts begin to learn more about healthy partner choice and find contentment in an ongoing relationship. You might start this process by making a list of *your* emotional needs and describe how those needs might best be met in a loving relationship. Then you can compare this list to your history of relationships—or to a current one—to get a sense of what you might do to get your healthy needs met. Emotional needs are experiences like:

- Feeling safe
- Feeling valued
- Feeling attended to
- Feeling appreciated
- Consistency
- Feeling acknowledged
- Feeling supported
- Feeling encouraged

Once you've written your list, you might find it useful to put the items on your list in order by priority. This exercise will help you to identify your most important needs first. Here's a sample exercise:

1. **My emotional need in a relationship:**
   To feel appreciated.
   How I know if this need is being met:
   If he noticed the things I do for him and thanks me. If he takes the time to do some things for me without my asking him to do so. He takes the time to tell me I look handsome or hot.

2. **My emotional need in a relationship:**
   To get physical affection.

How I know if this need is being met:
Lots of hugs, being held at night. Kissing and cuddling just for the sake of being close. Getting a big hug when I get home at night. Never being asked to watch porn during sex. Sex on a regular basis that is mutual.

3. My emotional need in a relationship:
To feel accepted.
How I know if this need is being met:
He doesn't agree with my criticisms about my body and seems to love me without judgment. Getting encouragement for the things that interest me. Not having to dress up for our time together or have any special reason to be together other than spending time.

4. My emotional need in a relationship:
To feel safe being myself with him.
How I know if this need is being met:
Being playful together and silly sometimes. He helps me out in difficult times and responds when I ask for help. He's accountable for his mistakes and remains honest. I don't have to wonder which issues belong to me and which issues belong to him.

Ways of knowing your needs are being met:
Your partner takes actions on a regular basis—often without being asked—that leave you with the feelings above.

Now make your own list:

1. My emotional need in a relationship:

How I know this need is being met:

2. My emotional need in a relationship:

How I know this need is being met:

3. My emotional need in a relationship:

How I know this need is being met:

4. My emotional need in a relationship:

How I know this need is being met:

5. My emotional need in a relationship:

How I know this need is being met:

Through exercises like these you can develop a better sense of what is truly important to you in friendships and partnership. This kind of insight and self-reflection allows you to enjoy the intensity of dating and sex, knowing that there can be something deeper as time goes by. Being familiar with your needs will help you determine if a particular relationship will serve you in a healthy way.

Pia Mellody offers more helpful words on unhealthy relationships:

> Many of us think that finding the right partner will complete a missing part of ourselves, finally making us feel whole. We also believe that this ideal lover will reveal the meaning of life to us. But each one of us has the potential to feel whole and fulfilled from within ourselves to the extent that we can develop our competence in self-love, self-protection, self-care, and self-containment. In addition, each one of us searches for and eventually finds the meaning of life for ourselves, rather than looking to our partner to reveal it to us. Our lives are ours; our partner's life is his or hers. No one can give us the ultimate answers for our own lives.

BREAKING THE CYCLE

As mentioned at the beginning of this chapter, many recovering sex addicts, unhappy with their sexual behavior and eager to find a healthier way to deal with their needfulness and compulsivity, flip from the desperate search for sex to the desperate search for love. This switch from one addiction to another leads them to conclude that neither sex nor love can bring them the connection and contentment they seek.

Recovery from the cycle of love addiction involves taking responsibility for a history of poor partner choices, lack of honesty, a habit of blaming the other individual, poor communication, and lack of self-care. Most important, the road to recovery begins with a willingness to tolerate the anxious need to be with someone without acting on that need for a period of time. Many recovering love addicts have had to commit to not dating or being sexual for 90 days or more to give themselves the time to learn how to meet their own emotional needs outside dating, romance, or sex.

For people who are already in a primary relationship, the path toward change and healing begins with meeting their emotional needs through the help of supportive others (therapists, 12-step groups, and reliable friends). One of the most valuable lessons to be learned at this point is how to stop shifting the blame for your unhappiness onto the shoulders of your partner.

Love addiction recovery requires rigorous education and self-examination to discover the characteristics of healthy relationships—which typically involves reading self-help books, writing recovery plans, and using a journal. Writing a thorough history of your past behavior around men, sexuality, and dating can also be very helpful. Exploring the underlying emotional conflicts that have provided the drive for unhealthy interactions in your relationship by attending therapy and 12-step programs will equip both partners to find new ways of relating and meeting each others' needs.

CHAPTER 9
BEYOND SEX AND LOVE ADDICTION: TAKING HEALTHY NEXT STEPS

MOVING ON

While we all have healthy needs for attention, validation, and intimacy, sex addicts use sex as a shortcut to get those needs met. These shortcuts—such as anonymous sex, affairs, or prostitutes—always feel powerfully fulfilling in the moment and provide a brief imitation of intimacy, but ultimately they only bring more feelings of emptiness rather than emotional nourishment.

Ed, whom we met at the beginning of this book, reflects on what he has learned in sexual sobriety:

> The one thing I never could stand—and the main reason I think I acted out so often—was loneliness. I could never tolerate long weekends, unplanned evenings, or times when I didn't have a lot of people around me. I just hated being alone.
>
> As independent as I always thought I was— not needing anyone, being able to walk away from any situation that wasn't working for me at a moment's notice—one of the first things I saw as I started therapy and stopped acting out sex-

ually was just how emotionally needy I really am. And I just hate that. In my mind I would rather not have to depend on anyone, but now it's so clear to me that all my cruising and the endless sex was just a desperate way to try to meet *emotional* needs, not physical ones. All those sex dates made me feel wanted, important, and valued, but without my taking any real emotional risks or having to make myself vulnerable in any real way.

Funny, though—while I was having sex with some hooker or a guy in the sauna, sometimes I would actually find myself thinking that I could get him to love me or rescue him. Sometimes while cruising the gym, I was half looking for sex and half somehow thinking I could find some man to know me and care about me.

Back then, even dating someone or finding a relationship didn't fulfill me because I never really let anyone in, never stayed around long enough or let anyone else stay around long enough, and I *always* lied and kept secrets. It took me a while to understand that despite all the sex I had been having and all the dates I had gone on, I really knew very little about what it all meant, primarily because I knew so little about what I really needed from the process.

Now that I'm getting better, I really feel sad for all the time and energy I lost wandering out there looking for something I never was going to find in my sexual hunt. I did sleep with some hot guys. But there are so very many things I could have been doing—so much of life I could have been enjoying—that I reserve some sadness in my heart for the me that could have been if I hadn't lost all of that time to sex.

SEX AND THE SINGLE GUY

When he decides to learn to develop healthy sexuality—whether he's single or in a relationship—the man healing from sex addiction must ensure that his new sexual experiences do more than serve as a quick fix. Since most addicts find it difficult in the moment to differentiate between intensity and intimacy, it's best to establish guidelines and boundaries before you get back in the scene to help yourself make good choices.

Rules of the Game

Whatever your politics or sociological beliefs regarding gay male sexuality, the simple truth is that sex addicts, regardless of sexual orientation, cannot sustain anonymous or casual patterns of sexual behavior without eventually descending into addictive sexual chaos and unhappiness. Bathhouses, public sex, phone sex lines, sex clubs, prostitutes, locker-room sex, and online hookups are all hot and exciting means of getting off and making sexual connections. Still, they *must* remain off-limits to gay sex addicts if they want to stay sexually sober, become "relationally responsible," and grow emotionally.

This said, a healthy sustainable sex life for gay male sex addicts should also involve sexuality that includes stable intimacy and a connection beyond the physical. This does not necessarily mean that the solution to sex addiction for the single guy is to find a boyfriend and "get married." In fact, in the early stages of recovery most sex addicts are fairly clueless about how to create and sustain the kind of healthy intimacy that's essential for a healthy long-term commitment.

Some people make the mistake of running out to find a relationship the minute they stop acting out sexually. Their immediate search for a partner becomes a means of avoiding emotional challenges (see the previous chapter on love addiction). However, for those single male sex addicts who have had some sober time and who are beginning to reengage sexually with others, there are **three dependable rules on which future healthy sex and dating in recovery rest**:

1) You have to get to know the man you are going to have sex with *before* you have sex with him.

2) Sex cannot be the *primary focus* of your dating or romantic encounters.

3) If being with a particular guy makes you feel bad (i.e. ,shameful, used, manipulated, or ignored) before, during, or after having sex, then it is probably not a good situation for you to continue—*no matter how good or exciting the sex is or how cute the guy might be.*

These three simple rules provide the most basic guide for avoiding a return to active sex addiction through dating. By following the rules, you can expect to begin to see signs of change in your behavior.

Some Examples of Change

1. If you've had a "fuck buddy" for many years, recovery from sex addiction doesn't necessarily mean you can never see him again—nor, for that matter, does it mean you can never be sexual with him again. Recovery *does* mean that if you're trying to heal from sex addiction, you don't just show up at your fuck buddy's house, have hot sex, then go home. *Recovering*

sex addicts who are working toward stability seek more emotional connection with those whom they choose to relate to through sex. A recovering sex addict might invite his former fuck buddy to go out and catch a movie (nonporn) *before* they have sex—or they might share a meal and/or spend the night together following sex. Neither of them may be interested in their becoming lovers or even dating, but the emphasis of their time together shifts from an exclusive focus on sex to a focus on relating, which may include sex.

2. And about that married guy who used to come over on the down-low for occasional hot sex and then run home to his wife and family, leaving you alone with a shower and a thank you? While you used to think this was a sizzling arrangement, in recovery this kind of relationship may no longer prove fulfilling. Now you begin to notice that each time he leaves, you feel lonelier than before he showed up. The playful fun you shared together becomes frustrating because you can't call him the next day, can't arrange more dates, or even reach out to him as a friend. This is not good for you—it just sets you up to want what you cannot have from the relationship. This is a situation you probably need to end.

3. And that trick who came over for "friendship" and sex but always seemed to need a few dollars from you every time? How has he always made you feel about yourself? You used to overlook your feelings by telling yourself you got something out of the relationship because he has such a great body. But in sexual recovery your priorities will begin to change from physical perfection to emotional self-care. So much for him!

SEX AND DATING

"When will I be ready to have sex? When can I start dating?" These are the questions single recovering sex addicts most often ask. Men who want to date or find a relationship need to differentiate **healthy dating** from simply using "dating" as an alternative means of finding sex.

Just as the sex addict beginning sobriety needs a well-defined written sexual boundary plan (see chapter 5), men who are starting to date should write a clear plan for dating. Below is a sample guide to help you learn new dating habits in recovery. This plan will not reflect everyone's needs, but as a typical example, it can help you devise your own recovery-friendly dating plan.

Sample Dating Plan
1. No sex until after the third date.
2. No sex during the first three weeks of knowing someone new.
3. On the first date we will stay in public places (we won't go into each other's houses or cars).
4. I don't date anyone that I wouldn't introduce to friends.
5. I don't date anyone who is in a relationship with someone else.
6. I don't date anyone who is actively using hard drugs.

In order to do this right, you should write out your own dating plan and discuss it with someone else in recovery, your sponsor, or your therapist. The goal of the dating plan is to help you learn how to get to know a guy before you're sexual with him. This supports your recovery because you begin to base your sexual choices not only on whether the guy's sexually exciting but also on whether you like something about *who he is*.

Dating plans help to tame the sex addict's initial impulse

to have sex before he ever gets to know the guy he is about to get off with. Most sex addicts will have sex with some cute guy they don't know in a heartbeat, but they're much less likely to tough it out to a third or fourth date with some jerk just to have sex.

Mario has just started dating in recovery:

> The dating part isn't so hard. I go out for coffee with him and see how we get along. If he's cute and if it works out, next time we do a movie or dinner. The hard part is that once I sit down and start talking to some of these guys—I mean really talking—my desire to sleep with them gets less and less intense. Most of them are fine until they open their mouths, and then I realize they don't have much to say.
>
> Since my dating plan says that I need to have three dates before having sex, I find that I just don't have that much sex. I've found in recovery that I really need to be stimulated by what a guy has to say before I want to be sexual with him. I know this is funny, but I never knew this before. When I was having anonymous sex, no one ever said anything—everything took place in silence. No wonder I could never make any of those situations work out. Now at least I have a real chance of feeling good about myself, getting laid, and finding a boyfriend.

Making a Dating Plan

Use the space on the next page to work on your own personal dating plan. As you're writing it, keep in mind both your goals for recovery and your past history of sexual acting out.

My Personal Dating Plan (Rules for Dating)

1)

2)

3)

4)

5)

6)

7)

8)

Name of the individual I discussed this with:

_____

Date on which I committed to my plan:

_____

My signature:

_____

ADVANCED DATING PLANS AND DATING SIGNPOSTS

One helpful exercise is to establish your own **Signposts of Dating**. These guidelines are designed to help remind you who is a good guy to date and who is bound to disappoint you. It's good to review this list with someone who can help you evaluate whether your expectations are reasonable or whether you're shortchanging yourself. Parts of the sample Signposts of Dating exercise below may work for you, so try to incorporate them into your recovery work. Or if some parts don't work, tinker with the exercise to make up your own personalized version. Some sample signposts of dating:

 Red Lights: These are characteristics or qualities that are *unacceptable to me* in anyone I might date. I would stop seeing him if he is:

1. An unrecovered drug addict or alcoholic
2. Still in a primary romantic relationship with someone else
3. Still living with an ex after they have broken up
4. An active sex addict
5. Someone who lies to me
6. Doesn't return my phone calls or e-mail
7. Unemployed with no other means of income
8. Closeted

 Yellow Lights: These characteristics or qualities might present a problem when I observe them in someone I am dating. I'll be cautious if he:

1. Talks about himself a lot more than he listens
2. Just ended a long-term relationship very recently
3. Only seems to call me when he needs something

4. Doesn't make me feel safe or appreciated when we're together

5. Makes me handle all the plans and contacts for socializing

6. Doesn't offer to pay for meals or dates

7. Doesn't seem to want me to meet any of his friends or coworkers

8. Doesn't want to plan ahead and often reschedules or cancels plans we've made

 Green Lights: These are characteristics or qualities in a potential romantic partner that I really like and find attractive. I would be encouraged to continue dating if he:

1. Tries to find out what is going on with me and how I am doing

2. Offers to help me out with things I am doing

3. Surprises me with fun or playful experiences

4. Has interesting hobbies and displays his own sense of creativity

5. Shares interests with me

6. Returns calls on time and shows up for things we've planned to do

NOW CREATE YOUR OWN PERSONAL SIGNPOSTS FOR DATING

By outlining the positive and negative signs that alert you to various personality types in dating and new relationships, you offer yourself a better opportunity for objective reflection when you're caught up in the excitement of meeting someone new. Having a solid plan to rely on makes it less likely that you will lose track of yourself in the intensity of the moment or become involved in painful or addictive relationships.

While nonaddicts may have the "common sense" to recognize these problems intuitively and respond to them in healthier ways, sex and love addicts need rational, well-defined guidelines to keep themselves grounded. While they may seem overly simplistic, these basic boundaries can help you successfully establish balanced relationships and genuine affection. As your sexual relationships become more selective and less casual, you'll begin to develop a better sense of whom to choose as a sexual partner, and you'll reflexively make healthier and safer choices about the individuals you date. Customizing your own plan will help you to establish some of these boundaries.

MY SIGNPOSTS FOR DATING

My Red Lights—He's a Goner!

1.

2.

3.

4.

5.

6.

My Yellow Lights—Maybe He's In, Maybe He's Out.

1.

2.

3.

4.

5.

6.

My Green Lights—This Guy's a Winner!

1.

2.

3.

4.

5.

6.

SPECIAL DATING RELATIONSHIPS: LEATHER, ROLE PLAY, FETISHES, AND B/D-S/M

As we saw in chapter 2, being involved in B/D-S/M, the leather scene, cross-dressing, or a fetish lifestyle does not make you a sex addict. It's not what body parts arouse you or how you touch or engage those parts that define sex addiction. Sex addiction is about shame, consequences, secrets, and isolation.

So how can a recovering sex addict who is into bondage, for example, experience his recovery *and* his healthy sexuality without feeling constrained by some of the more "vanilla" suggestions in this chapter? How can the more "alternative" sexual behaviors that rely on forms of objectification and intensity sustain a commitment to recovery? The answer: Go slow!

The word *recovery* literally means to retrieve or get back— not remove or subtract. The whole idea of sex addiction recovery implies that at some point the sex addict will be able to "recover" that which he has lost to his addiction. For the fetishist or masochist, this means that he'll be able to find ways to slowly integrate some of his past sexual activities back into his active sex life *provided* that they don't lead him back into serious consequences, shame, or self-hatred.

This reintegration proceeds imperfectly at first, but by using the help of his recovery support network, the B/D-S/M scenester or fetish enthusiast will be able to develop modes of sexual expression that reflect his deepest desires and support his sexual sobriety. As long as he's not sexually offending, it's essential that he not let anyone in the 12-step programs—or therapy professionals, for that matter—convince him that his sexual interests are wrong or pathological. If the sex addict's expression of his sexuality doesn't betray the basic recovery principals of not causing adverse consequences, not keeping secrets, not being abusive, not causing shame, and not engaging in nonconsensual activities, chances are any sex addict's behavior is supporting his sexual sobriety.

SEX AND THE RECOVERING COUPLE

Once again, Juan talks about what the recovery process has meant for him and his lover:

> After I disclosed all the acting out I had done, I was certain that our relationship would be over. For a while there it was pretty touch-and-go. Jeremy didn't even want to speak to me and asked me to move out for a couple of weeks. We talked seriously about splitting up.
>
> But with the help of some really good therapy, the support of our friends, and my recovery program, we made it past that first difficult period of time. There had always been a lot of love between us—despite my acting out—and we still wanted to explore that love to see where it went. We concluded that we're both reasonably good guys with problems that can be fixed if we really work at it. And we *have* been working at it.
>
> We remain committed to each other and we're slowly working through the hurt and broken trust. There have been new moments of what feels like real intimacy between us—some sexual, some physical, some just plain closeness. It's interesting because I feel so grateful now for the simplest exchanges between us—moments that I used to ignore or take for granted. When I reflect back on the past year of recovery, I feel like I've been given another chance to love.

REBUILDING TRUST IN A RELATIONSHIP

Sexual recovery for people in long-term relationships differs from healing as a single man because a relationship is a system that's already in place and requires special attention. Once trust in a relationship has been violated, the relationship is never quite the same. That is simply an unalterable fact of life.

Though a couple may mature after the trauma of addiction—and certainly relationships can continue—both partners must commit themselves to a rebuilding process that often proceeds in fits and starts as each partner grows in different ways and at a different paces.

For example, sex addicts in the early part of the recovery process are usually focused on specific tasks such as learning about sexual sobriety, attending support meetings, writing, or attending therapy. They may be feeling hopeful about finally having found a path that offers a way beyond their cycle of sexual acting-out. Spouses, however, are often in a very different emotional place. Even if they're also educating themselves about addiction and recovery, they're likely to feel angry, resentful, and mistrustful.

Unlike the addict—who has always known about his problem (even if only because of his persistent unhappiness) and feels some relief at the prospect of a possible solution—most spouses have been in the dark. Suddenly, they must face a problem they didn't want and didn't know they had. They may not be so glad to have found a "solution" because they may not have known that there was a problem in the first place!

Even in relationships where both partners have been sexually active with other people and betrayal of trust is not an issue, the nonaddicted spouse now has to contend with the loss of a playmate who has decided to "reform his ways." The addict is now questioning every aspect of his sexuality and setting boundaries and limits on his behavior at every turn. This is likely not what the nonmonogamous spouse bargained for when the two first paired up. In most cases, this volatile early period of recovery will pass as both partners adjust to new dynamics and stressors—and almost all relationships improve if the sex addict stays in recovery.

MONOGAMY

In a relationship where one or both partners may have a problem with sex addiction, new rules and boundaries may need to be created where none existed before. *If a couple wants to remain together, any scenario other than monogamy is not recommended, given the problems that casual sexual activity outside the relationship can present for sex addicts.* Many addictive couples have unconsciously avoided the intimacy and intensity that monogamy creates by never having a definitive conversation around "the monogamy question," or by choosing to remain an "open" couple. When a sex addict in a partnership chooses to recover, this indeterminacy or "openness" must end.

Both partners must commit to a higher degree of accountability and communication than ever before—in part because they will no longer have the excitement of sex partners outside their relationship to distract them from difficult emotions. For couples who have talked about but not committed to monogamy—where one or both partners have betrayed the other's trust—the healing process can transform a difficult period of hurt into a new opportunity for romantic and sexual intimacy.

RELATIONSHIP DYNAMICS AND SEXUAL ACTING-OUT

Sexual acting-out is triggered by both the addict's inability to tolerate difficult feelings and by relationship interactions that mirror childhood trauma. Recovering sex addicts in long-term relationships have to focus not only on their own recovery but also on emotional challenges as they arise in their intimate relationships. Just as the single man needs to understand more about his healthy wants and needs as he is starting to date, men in primary relationships need to identify what's reasonable to expect of their partners and find ways of communicating those needs.

When they were acting out, lying, and keeping secrets from their mates, most sex addicts never felt they had the right to assert themselves or their needs to their partners. In recovery, the addict must learn to be more stable, honest, and reliable, and this involves finding ways to identify and express his feelings and needs. Active sex addicts in long-term relationships often "play the victim"—they justify their sexual behavior by blaming their spouses. "He doesn't listen to me! Why shouldn't I get it some somewhere else?" In sobriety, the recovering sex addict can no longer place responsibility for his sexual acting-out on his partner. Instead he has to be accountable for his own emotions and actions. He must also learn to be assertive in his intimate relationships.

Tommy, who has been in a relationship with Jon for seven years, explains how he developed a healthy sense of personal accountability:

> I used to blame Jon for a lot of my acting out. He wasn't there for me, he asked too much of me, and on and on. Now I know that not only did I use that kind of thinking to justify my going out with other guys, but I also never understood that I could have a say in how things went in our relationship.
>
> For some reason related to my childhood issues, I never stood up to Jon, never really talked

much about what I wanted, and usually just did what he wanted. But when I didn't get something, I would just sulk, retreat from him, and go act out. Now, through going to meetings, getting therapy, and doing couples communication work with Jon, I'm learning to take more responsibility for what I want and feel. I have to take more risks to say what I want and need—even disagree or risk arguing—if that's what it takes to make sure I feel heard by him.

I may not always get my way, or I might only get a compromise, but at least I'm starting to assert myself. As I've done this, my desire to act out has diminished significantly. We're also starting to establish a new experience of loving sexuality and playfulness that we never had before—not even when we first met.

RELATIONSHIP SEXUALITY

Today's psychologists and sexologists are busily exploring successful long-term heterosexual marriages to try to learn what many gay men have long intuitively known: Couples can maintain an exciting sex life by frequently introducing new forms of sexual and sensual stimulation. So the "new" advice goes out to the heterosexual world on every pop magazine cover: "Take Sexy Weekend Spa Holidays!" "Try Toys!" "Scents!" "Lubricants!" "Lingerie!"

An early goal for recovering sex addicts, however, is to move away from sexual innovation and focus on emotional closeness and physical intimacy. It's a major challenge—perhaps as difficult as eliminating the sexual acting-out itself—for sex addicts to strike this balance between ongoing healthy intimacy and maintaining genuine sexual arousal and excitement.

The recovery prescription for many gay couples with a sex addiction problem is just the opposite of the (secondhand) advice for nonaddicted heterosexuals: *Put away the distractions and concentrate on each other.* One of the first steps toward healthy sexuality for gay male couples is to discard the porn, the drugs, the toys, and sometimes even the genital- or orgasm-focused experience for a time and exchange it for simple connection and arousal. This kind of intimacy involves simple touching, caressing, and eye contact.

Through these careful, deliberate expressions couples can build romantic closeness and sexual trust—perhaps for the first time. They may later decide to reintroduce toys and other distractions, but before they make that decision they must establish a foundation of intimacy.

The following lists contain some suggestions for building intimacy. Experiment with some options of your own, and consult other couples in recovery for more suggestions.

Nonphysical Romantic Intimacy Building Blocks

- Love letters
- Special names for each other
- Gifts—both small and large
- Flowers
- Making dates to spend time together
- Taking time to listen
- Taking time to do things he likes more than you do *without looking for compliments*
- Doing favors for your partner
- Taking over a task he hates (dishes, laundry) *without looking for compliments*
- Looking into his eyes
- Telling him what you value about him—*giving* compliments

- Going dancing together
- Walking in nature together
- Planning special evenings, weekends alone or with friends
- Coming home early

Physical Romantic Intimacy Building Blocks
- Bathing each other
- Massaging his back
- Combing his hair
- Rubbing his feet
- Holding hands
- Kissing
- Cuddling

Sexual Intimacy Building Blocks
- Talking during sex—letting your partner know more about what you like.
- Keeping the lights on—looking into his eyes as you pleasure him.
- Allowing laughter—sex doesn't have to be so serious!
- Staying present—being willing to stop if you get distracted.
- Being spontaneous—trying new positions and being playful with each other.
- Learning more about male sexuality through reading or workshops.

INTIMACY HOMEWORK

Using the suggestions above, take some time to interview your partner and ask him what experiences and activities make him feel special in each area. Be sure to take notes. Then have your partner interview you. This exercise will give both of you insights that will enrich the romantic and sexual qualities that are unique your relationship. Make dates to repeat the exercise.

LIFE IN RECOVERY: BOREDOM OR BLISS?

While most sex addicts enter 12-step recovery or treatment to find relief from the suffering their addiction has caused them, they usually aren't prepared for the necessary behavioral changes and emotional discomfort the process often entails. Though they may have accepted that they have a problem, some addicts still balk at having to dramatically alter attitudes they previously held dear. Almost all of them struggle to deal with larger daily concerns—like overworking, poor exercise and eating, overspending, alcohol and drug use, problem relationships, or isolation—that can easily restart the addictive process if addicts don't attend to them vigilantly.

No sex addict has ever managed to remain sober simply because he felt terrible about the consequences of his sexual acting-out—no matter how awful the consequences. The bad feelings from traumatic events fade over time, but the lure of sexual intensity never loses its potency. Maintaining sexual sobriety means carefully practicing a way of living that allows you to pursue long-term fulfillment that involves healthier habits and relationships.

A common concern of recovering sex addicts who stick with the process over the long haul is that a life without sexual abandon can seem kind of boring. "Isn't life too predictable without the thrilling risks of sexual adventuring, sport fucking, and the drama of high-maintenance relationships?" What to do with all the time you formerly devoted to chasing after volatile, mind-blowing sex?

Since a primary goal of recovery is to distance yourself from intensity-based sexual and romantic experiences, it's really helpful to introduce yourself to experiences of serenity and mindfulness. Exploring quieting practices such as yoga, meditation, journaling, and artistic self-reflection offers essential tools to help you capture and sustain calm, quiet feelings. The more you learn to recognize, contain, and manage strong emotions, the healthier you become. Many people choose to incorporate some type of spiritual or religious practice into their recovery, though the form that practice takes varies widely from individual to individual.

There are also many ways to develop creative intensity that will enliven your life and relationships without taking you down the wrong road. Trying out new hobbies, following your work or creative dreams, and engaging in sports or other activities that you had previously denied yourself all allow you to be more open without risking self-destruction.

Often, finding ways to contribute to the well-being of others—rather than simply working to get something for yourself—brings self-esteem. Again Ed speaks of his experience:

> I'm amazed by the unexpected changes that sexual recovery has made in my life. When I was younger, I loved playing with my cousins and the other kids in my neighborhood. Now that I'm not at the gym every night cruising for hours, I take the time to volunteer at the children's hospital, working with families and the kids there who need so much attention and care. It makes me feel worthwhile, and I have a lot of fun with it.
>
> I have retaught myself to cook pretty well too—something I always loved—and I've been hosting monthly get-togethers for a group of guys from my recovery group. I go to a poker night for the single gay guys I know where each of us makes

sure to invite at least one other single friend as a potential match for our friends.

I'm not having any hot sex yet, and so far there's no "right guy," but I'm having a lot of unexpected fun and I'm growing. The desire for sexual intensity that I thought would never leave has mostly waned, and I'm very grateful for that. So many good things have happened since I first realized I had to deal with my sex addiction.

Surprising though it may be to the sex addict who has not entered recovery, life without the endless pursuit of sexual intensity can be filled with wonderful experiences and plenty of fun. As sex addicts withdraw from their patterns of acting out and grieve the loss of sex as a distraction from their troubles, they discover they have much more time and energy for creativity and personal growth, making what might initially have seemed boring not so dull after all. Beyond 12-step recovery, the urban gay world has countless opportunities for play and creative expression that have nothing to do with sex. Activities abound—from softball teams and theater groups to meditation and gay rodeo.

"Hopeful" is a better word than "boring" to describe the life of a gay man who has decided to move beyond the objectification, shame, and secrecy of sex addiction. It really is possible to escape lifelong patterns of addictive sexual behavior and change your life! This is a fact. Men are doing it every day. No matter how long you've been living in a cycle of addiction and no matter how profound the consequences of your acting out have been, you can begin to change your life *today*. The only tools you need are the willingness to be honest, the motivation to change, and the ongoing involvement of people who understand the problem and are also working toward healing.

NOTES

Chapter 1
1. The addiction cycle was adapted from multiple sources originating from the work of Patrick J. Carnes and Mark Laaser.
2. The G-SAST was developed by Robert Weiss and Patrick J. Carnes.

Chapter 3
1. Patrick J. Carnes, *Out of the Shadows,* 3rd ed. (Center City, Minn.: Hazelden, 2001), pp. 112-115.
2. Graeme Hanson and Lawrence Hartmann. "Latency Development in Prehomosexual Boys," *The Textbook of Homosexuality and Mental Health* (Washington, D.C.: American Psychiatric Association, 1996), passim.

Chapter 4
1. Patrick J. Carnes, *Contrary to Love* (Minneapolis: CompCare, 1989) passim.
2. R.P. Cabaj, "Substance Abuse in the Gay and Lesbian Community," *Substance Abuse: A Comprehensive Textbook,* ed. Joyce H. Lowinson et al., 2nd ed., (Philadelphia: Lippincott, Williams & Wilkins, 1992), pp. 852-860.
3. R.P. Cabaj, "Substance Abuse in Gay Men, Lesbians, and Bisexuals," *Homosexuality and Mental Health,* ed. R.P. Cabaj and Terry S. Stein (Washington, D.C.:

American Psychiatric Association, 1996), pp. 783-800.

4. Cathy Reback, *The Social Construction of a Gay Drug: Methamphetamine Use Among Gay Men in Los Angeles* (Los Angeles: City of Los Angeles AIDS Office, 1997), p. 49.

5. Reback, p. 48.

6. Interview with Joni Lavick, Director of Mental Health Services, Los Angeles Gay & Lesbian Center, November 2003.

7. DSM IV TR (Arlington, VA: American Psychiatric Association, 2000), passim. Adapted from the criteria for substance abuse and substance dependency.

8. As adapted from the identifying checklists of S-Anon and COSA.

Chapter 5

1. Patrick J. Carnes, *Out of the Shadows,* 1st ed. (Minneapolis: CompCare, 1983), passim.

Chapter 7

1. As utilized by several of the 12-step sexual recovery programs, specifically Sex Addicts Anonymous and Sexual Compulsives Anonymous.

Chapter 8

1. Pia Mellody, with Andrea Wells Miller and J. Keith Miller, *Facing Love Addiction: Giving Yourself the Power to Change the Way You Love* (San Francisco: Harper, 1992), passim.

APPENDIX 1
RESOURCES FOR SUPPORT

Below are selected listings of organizations for sex addicts and sex offenders as well as couples in which one or both partners are sexually addicted. Many meetings held under the auspices of these organizations are open to anyone who wishes to attend, while others are closed to members only or are gender-specific. Before attending a meeting, it's best to check ahead by calling a local hotline number for a particular organization; this will help you determine the best meeting for your needs. Hotline operators usually take your name and number and then call you back with meeting information or forward a recorded announcement. Your conversations with hotline staff remain confidential.

12-STEP PROGRAMS FOR SEX ADDICTS

Sex Addicts Anonymous (SAA): www.sexaa.org
National: (800) 477-8191

A 12-step program for sex addicts and some sex offenders, SAA offers a good mix of gay- and straight-oriented meetings. Women attend some meetings.

Sexual Compulsives Anonymous (SCA): www.sca-recovery.org
National: (800) 977-4325 (977-HEAL)

A 12-step program designed primarily for sex addicts, SCA

is concentrated mostly in major urban areas. Its meetings often reflect a sizable gay presence. Women attend some meetings.

Sex and Love Addicts Anonymous (SLAA): www.slaafws.org
National: (781) 255-8825

A 12-step program designed for sex addicts and individuals with patterns of unhealthy romantic relationships, SLAA has a greater female presence than many other recovery programs. Some meetings are for women only.

Sexaholics Anonymous (SA): www.sa.org
National: (866) 424-8777

SA is a 12-step program for sex addicts and sex offenders. Most of the meetings are composed of men. The least gay-supportive of the 12-step recovery programs for sex addiction, SA bases its definition of sobriety on traditional concepts of marriage. But individual groups vary widely in their degree of openness to GLBT issues.

Sexual Recovery Anonymous (SRA): www.sexualrecovery.org

SRA is a 12-step program similar to SA, except that the phrase "committed relationship" is used instead of "marriage." Meetings are limited in number but open to everyone in sexual recovery. Regional contact numbers for groups in the United States and abroad can be found at SRA's Web site.

12-STEP PROGRAMS FOR SPOUSES

S-Anon International: www.sanon.org
National: (615) 833-3152

A companion program to SA, S-Anon is a 12-step program for spouses/partners of sex addicts and sex offenders. Most meetings are primarily made up of married women.

COSA: www.cosa-recovery.org
National: (763) 537-6904

A companion program to SAA, COSA is a 12-step program for partners and significant others of sex addicts and sex offenders. Both men and women attend groups.

12-STEP PROGRAMS FOR COUPLES

Recovering Couples Anonymous (RCA): www.recovering-couples.org
(510) 663-2312

This 12-step program is national in scope and focuses on recovery issues experienced by couples affected by sex addiction. Both partners (addict and co-addict) are encouraged to attend. All committed couples are welcome.

NATIONAL THERAPY RESOURCES

Sex Help: www.sexhelp.com
On online resource developed by Dr. Patrick Carnes. Offers books, exercises, and referrals from the leader in the field.

The Society for the Advancement of Sexual Health (SASH): www.sash.net
(770) 989-9754

Formerly known as the National Council for Sexual Addiction and Compulsivity, SASH serves both treatment professionals and recovering individuals. Provides resources and information on addiction therapists, treatment centers, and support groups.

The Sexual Recovery Institute: www.sexualrecovery.com
(310) 360-0130
A treatment center in Southern California, under the direction of the author, providing local and national outpatient programs. Visit the Web site to find helpful articles and referrals.

APPENDIX 2
RECOMMENDED READING

FOR SEX AND LOVE ADDICTS

Carnes, Patrick J. *A Gentle Path Through the Twelve Steps: The Classic Guide for All People in the Process of Recovery.* Rev ed. Center City, Minn: Hazelden, 1994. A thorough workbook designed to help people in recovery work on the steps in written form with clear outlines and direction.

Carnes, Patrick J. *Out of the Shadows: Understanding Sexual Addiction.* 3rd ed. Center City, Minn.: Hazelden, 1983. Over 20 years ago, Carnes's groundbreaking book first introduced the idea of sex addiction into popular culture. The latest edition is as helpful and current as ever. Though written primarily with heterosexual readers in mind, it is a must-read for every recovering sex addict.

Hope and Recovery: A Twelve-Step Guide for Healing from Compulsive Sexual Behavior. Rev. ed. Center City, Minn.: Hazelden, 1994. This was one of the first books to comprehensively describe the application of the principles of Alcoholics Anonymous to sex addiction and sexual compulsion. It includes a wide range of personal stories in which recovering sex addicts share their experiences and hopes.

Kasl, Charlotte. *If the Buddha Dated: A Handbook for Finding Love on a Spiritual Path.* New York: Penguin, 1999. Dr. Kasl's first exploration of helping single individuals find a grace-based way to date and seek a mate is a wonderful read and an instructive guide to healthy, recovery-oriented dating.

Kort, Joe. *10 Smart Things Gay Men Can Do to Improve Their Lives.* Los Angeles: Alyson Books, 2003. Gay psychotherapist Joe Kort brings his experience of working with hundreds of clients to his book, which details 10 powerful and positive steps that gay men can take to achieve a healthier, more rewarding life.

Maltz, Wendy. *The Sexual Healing Journey: A Guide for Survivors of Sexual Abuse.* Rev. ed. New York: HarperCollins, 2001. This step-by-step guide to recovery from sexual abuse offers first-person accounts of women and men at every stage of the sexual healing journey and includes exercises and techniques for survivors of sexual abuse.

Mellody, Pia, with Andrea Wells Miller and J. Keith Miller. *Facing Love Addiction: Giving Yourself the Power to Change the Way You Love.* San Francisco: Harper, 1992. A classic introductory discussion of love addiction and learning to understand and heal from its challenges.

Sex and Love Addicts Anonymous. Norwood, Mass.: Augustine Fellowship, 1986. The official book of the 12-step program of Sex and Love Addicts Anonymous. A vital resource of understanding for love addicts.

FOR PARTNERS/FRIENDS AND FAMILY

Beattie, Melody. *Codependent No More: How to Stop Controlling Others and Start Caring for Yourself.* Center City, Minn.:

Hazelden, 1987. Recovery has begun for millions of individuals with this straightforward guide. Through therapeutic exercises and examples drawn from real-life experiences, Beattie shows how controlling individuals can force those close to them to lose sight of their own needs and happiness.

Corley, M. Deborah and Jennifer Schneider. *Disclosing Secrets: When, to Whom, and How Much to Reveal.* Center City, Minn.: Hazelden, 2001. "We are only as sick as the secrets we keep": This central tenet of recovery from addiction celebrates the liberating, healing experience of disclosure. But the actual process of revealing sensitive secrets related to addiction can be difficult, even excruciating. Taking a straightforward step-by-step approach, Jennifer Schneider and Debra Corley help readers to discern the kinds of information that are advisable to share as well as to develop a plan for constructive disclosure.

Schneider, Jennifer P., and Robert Weiss. *Cybersex Exposed: Simple Fantasy or Obsession?* Center City, Minn.: Hazelden, 2001. Cowritten by the author of *Cruise Control* and Jennifer Schneider, an expert on partner and spousal concerns, this book primarily focuses on cybersex addiction and is intended for individuals of all sexual orientations. Taking a reality-based approach, it does a good job of discussing the problem of cybersex addiction and potential solutions.

FOR THERAPISTS AND PROFESSIONALS

Carnes, Patrick J. *Contrary to Love: Helping the Sexual Addict.* Center City, Minn.: Hazelden, 1989. This helpful, understated book is a good read for any clinician wanting to better understand how to approach the treatment of a sex addict.

Carnes, Patrick J. *Facing the Shadow: Starting Sexual and Relationship Recovery.* Center City, Minn: Hazelden, 2001. This task-centered book guides individuals through the recovery process with written assignments and psychoeducation.

Carnes, Patrick J., and Kenneth M. Adams, eds. *Clinical Management of Sex Addiction.* New York: Brunner-Routledge, 2002. A variety of experts offer their perspectives on sex addiction in this compendium of articles, many of which are practical in focus and offer helpful suggestions about dealing with day-to-day issues and administering patient care.

Coombs, Robert Holman, ed. *Handbook of Addictive Disorders: A Practical Guide to Diagnosis and Treatment.* Hoboken, N.J.: Wiley, 2004. This extremely helpful guide to understanding all types of addictions and how to manage them was compiled by experts in all the various areas of addiction treatment. It is the first comprehensive work of its kind.

Cooper, Al, ed. *Sex and the Internet: A Guidebook for Clinicians.* New York: Brunner-Routledge, 2002. This is the first professional book covering issues related to sex and the Internet. Leading scholars, clinicians, and academicians in the field have contributed to this emerging and often misunderstood topic.

FOR COUPLES

Berzon, Betty. *Permanent Partners: Building Gay and Lesbian Relationships That Last.* Los Angeles: Plume Books, 1990. Berzon offers readers a well-written and authoritative guide to creating healthy, lasting partnerships. She has drawn upon more than 15 years of professional experience counseling lesbians and gay men.

Carnes, Patrick J., Debra Laaser, and Mark Laaser. *Open Hearts: Renewing Relationships with Recovery, Romance, and Reality.* Wickenburg, Ariz.: Gentle Path Press, 1999. A task-focused book designed to take couples through the recovery process with written assignments and homework.

Hendrix, Harville. *Getting the Love You Want: A Guide for Couples.* New York: Owl Books, 2001. Now available in reprint, Hendrix's classic guide covers how to understand and confront patterns of problem behavior that couples enact over and over again.

Kasl, Charlotte. *If the Buddha Married: Creating Enduring Relationships on a Spiritual Path.* New York: Penguin, 2001. This is a lovely book offering kind wisdom and direction for any couple wishing to move beyond relationship intensity onto a path of intimacy.

Larsen, Earnie. *Stage II Relationships: Love Beyond Addiction.* San Francisco: Harper, 1987. Larsen discusses how couples and families can rebuild relationships and intimacy after confronting issues of addiction.

Marcus, Eric. *The Male Couple's Guide: Finding a Man, Making a Home, Building a Life*, 3rd ed. New York: Perennial Currents, 1999. A warm, commonsense book offering help for all stages of gay dating and relationships.

Schaeffer, Brenda. *Is It Love or Is It Addiction?* 2nd ed. Center City, Minn.: Hazelden, 1997. Schaeffer's book is useful for gaining an understanding of the distinctions between addictive and nonaddictive relationships. She also offers suggestions on how to improve relationships.

AUTHOR'S NOTE

The idea for this book finds its root in an article I wrote about 10 years ago called "Treatment Concerns for Gay Male Sex Addicts" (which was subsequently published in *Sexual Addiction and Compulsivity: The Journal of Treatment and Prevention*). In that article I hoped to speak to the need for therapists who treat sex addicts to understand the specific language and experiences of gay men who compulsively act out in an addictive manner through sexual behavior. Although the underlying psychological dynamic that drives some men to act out sexually is pretty much the same regardless of sexual orientation, therapists must understand gay men's distinct patterns of behavior and modes of expression if they are to help gay sex addicts confront their denial and begin to build healthier ways of coping. In sex addiction, as in so much else, it's a mistake to think of heterosexual experience as "normal" or "normative."

At the time, I wrote the article in a straightforward attempt to provide other professionals with information I had gleaned over many years of clinical work with gay male sex addicts. As these thoughts continued to develop after the article was written, I started to attend conferences and speak at professional events to introduce the concerns of sexually addicted gay men into general lectures about sex addiction. I also began to listen closely to my peers in the mental health field. I was surprised to hear their private apprehension around openly discussing and writing about gay mental health, gay addiction, and gay sexual problems—primarily because they feared ostracism from conservatives outside the gay community and charges of homophobia from activists within it. This double bind convinced me of the urgent need to speak out openly about the mental health challenges gay men face so that men with problems can get the help and information they need.

It is more important to provide information to those in need than to protect an idealized image of gay sexual freedom or to try to avoid a backlash from people who want to push a homophobic political agenda. Addiction professionals and recovering people know that the unhealthy family avoids talking about its problems in order to look "normal" or to avoid criticism. The family only becomes increasingly more dysfunctional when it fails to examine its problems honestly. This is true for any community of people.

Since the late 1970s the book *Out of the Shadows* and other extraordinary work by Dr. Patrick Carnes have served as the primary gateway to truth and healing for nearly every male sex addict—though when reading that work most gay men had to interpret their experiences through a heterosexual lens. Female sex addicts, both gay and straight, have had the good fortune to have Charlotte Kasl's fine book, *Women, Sex, and Addiction,* available to them. It is my hope that *Cruise Control* will help gay and bisexual sex addicts and their partners to truly see themselves, begin to understand their experience, and take their first steps on the road to recovery.

Robert Weiss, L.C.S.W., C.A.S.
—Los Angeles